SAFEGUARDING ADULTS ONLINE
Perspectives on Rights to Participation

Emma Bond and Andy Phippen

D1612786

P

First published in Great Britain in 2022 by

Policy Press, an imprint of
Bristol University Press
University of Bristol
1-9 Old Park Hill
Bristol
BS2 8BB
UK
t: +44 (0)117 374 6645
e: bup-info@bristol.ac.uk

Details of international sales and distribution partners are available at policy.bristoluniversitypress.co.uk

© Bristol University Press 2022

British Library Cataloguing in Publication Data
A catalogue record for this book is available from the British Library

ISBN 978-1-4473-6057-5 hardcover
ISBN 978-1-4473-6058-2 paperback
ISBN 978-1-4473-6059-9 ePub
ISBN 978-1-4473-6060-5 ePdf

Cover design: Nicky Borowiec
Front cover image: © travelguide/Adobe Stock
Bristol University Press and Policy Press use environmentally responsible print partners.
Printed in Great Britain by CMP, Poole

Contents

List of figures and tables

Figures

Tables

Acknowledgements

The authors would like to thank James Codling, Mental Capacity Act and Deprivation of Liberty Safeguards Training and Development Manager, Cambridgeshire County Council, and Alex Ruck Keene, a barrister at 39 Essex Chambers who specialises in mental capacity and mental health law, and creator of the http://www.mentalcapacitylawandpolicy.org.uk/ blog, for their time, knowledge and interest in this book. We had many detailed conversations with them around all aspects of adult online safeguarding during the production of this book and continue to learn a great deal from them.

1

Introduction

Scope, content and aims

While the concept of online safeguarding for children and young people is well explored from both research and policy perspectives, and there are many statutory requirements on stakeholders to ensure effective training and education in this arena, the same cannot be said for adults with learning difficulties and mental capacity issues, and those supporting them. This book fills a long-recognised gap in the online safeguarding arena and has been written for a multi-disciplinary and a multi-agency audience, including academics, practitioners and policy makers. It is apparent that currently there is a dearth of academic research, policy direction or practice guidance related to these difficulties and challenges, leaving those with safeguarding responsibilities for 'vulnerable adults' to make poorly informed judgements on their capacity to engage with online services and confusion as to how best to support them.

We deliberately use the quotation marks around 'vulnerable adults' because it is a term not without its problems. The *No Secrets* statutory guidance (Department of Health, 2000), which we will discuss in more detail later in this text, attempted to address adult safeguarding, using a broad definition of a 'vulnerable adult' as someone who 'is or may be in need of community care services by reason of mental or other disability, age or illness; and who is or may be unable to take care of him or herself, or unable to protect him or herself against significant harm or exploitation'. The Care Act 2014 (UK Government, 2014) has superseded this, and section 42 of this act no longer refers specifically to vulnerable adults, instead defining factors that might make an adult vulnerable:

(a) has care and support needs;
(b) is experiencing or is at risk of abuse or neglect; and
(c) is unable to protect themselves from that abuse or neglect because of their care and support needs.

Nevertheless, a point often missed is that vulnerability is such an intangible term to tie down, yet used so frequently by policy makers, the press and even professionals. As Oxford academic Herring (2016) so clearly explores in his book *Vulnerable Adults and the Law*, '[e]veryone is vulnerable'. He further explores the transient nature of vulnerability and how external factors can increase or decrease an individual's vulnerability in any given context. An adult with learning difficulties or a brain injury is not, purely as a result of having a learning difficulty or brain injury, at risk of harm. However, the learning difficulty might cause their risk of harm to increase disproportionately compared to an adult without learning difficulties in certain events, such as being scammed online. However, we would stress once more that this would depend on many factors, such as the nature of the learning difficulty, the individual's experience online and education they have obtained about online harms, and the quality of support the receive.

To reiterate, every decision should be based upon the individual, not a broad concept of vulnerability or categorisation of risk as a result of disability.

It has been deeply concerning to us and to others for many years that the importance given to ensuring that children and young people have the knowledge and skills to engage with the digital environment has not been afforded to other groups of society deemed vulnerable. In his introduction to *A Sociology of Monsters*, John Law (1991: 1) eloquently argued that:

> [w]e founded ourselves on class; then, at a much later date we learned a little more about ethnicity; more recently still we learned something – perhaps not very much yet- about age and disability. So might a white, middle aged man with a normatively approved set of physical skills write of the history of his sociology. So might he comment on the way in which he slowly learned that 'his' sociology had never spoken for 'us': that all along the sociological 'we' was a Leviathan that had achieved its (sense of order) by usurping or silencing the other voices.

We hope that this book will begin to address this and provide a useful and thought-provoking analysis to underpin a holistic and person-centred approach to online safeguarding that respects people's rights to online participation and to privacy.

Our analysis centres mainly on judgments emerging from the Court of Protection (discussed in far more detail in Chapter 4), the online safeguarding challenges arising from the judgments presented, and arguments around capacity to engagement with the internet and social media as a result. Due to this focus, guided by the judgments of the Court of Protection, we are drawn in the main towards vulnerable adults with a learning disability or brain injury, and, we would observe, mainly younger adults. Clearly, this is not the only type of online harm affecting vulnerable adults in our society, and we hear many anecdotes of older people with, for example, dementia being subject to online scams and financial fraud. While the literature in this area remains sparser and indeed contradictory around the prevalence of this (for example see Grimes et al, 2010; Van Wilson, 2013; Ross et al, 2014), it is not something we wish to deliberately exclude through lack of interest.

Rather, the focus of this type of online harm falls outside of the scope of a monograph that uses Court of Protection judgments as a core source of evidence. Cases of scamming and online fraud do not result in claims around capacity to engage with the internet and social media as a result. As we will explore in this text, the focus tends to be more on sexual and criminal behaviours.

We draw extensively on the 2019 ruling by Cobb J in the Court of Protection cases *Re A* [2019] EWCOP 2 and *Re B* [2019] EWCOP 3 throughout this text. The ruling, regarding two adults with capacity issues, is central to the text to understand the legal perspectives in the UK which have raised considerable interest in the rights of people to access digital services and social interaction online. We also provide an in-depth exploration of how professionals with a duty of care might balance safeguarding with inalienable rights of those individuals to go online unless it is not in their best interests to do so. In the ruling, Cobb J states that engaging with online services is a distinct safeguarding concern. He defines a list of six *tests* for determining whether adults are capable of understanding safeguarding issues when online, and he proposes this guidance be used by those making mental capacity assessments on individuals.

However, our analysis, particularly against the body of knowledge related to the online safeguarding of children and young people would suggest that, first, while the guidance was initially welcomed, its foundations in Livingstone and Haddon's (2009) 3Cs of online safety adopt an out of date, non-inclusive perspective of the passive consumer, rather than acknowledging the concept of *agency* and the *diversity* of lived experience for individuals who are making choices when engaging in behaviours online which may deemed as *risky*. More recently, both *independence* and *choice* have become central elements in the development of new forms of service delivery for all adult social care user groups (Fyson and Kitson, 2010). Such choices may be indeed by constrained by structure and limited or they may be better informed according to the level of professional and personal support individuals may have. Thus, the context of the social or professional *network* available to the individual can be either an unhelpful/restrictive one or play a supportive/facilitating role in that individual's life. This contextual network is often overlooked or ignored in deterministic discourses which privilege protection over participation rights. As such, the guidance as it stands sets the bar for assessing capacity extremely high in its presumption that capacity is challenged (for example section 1 Mental Capacity Act 2005 – MCA), and many adults without capacity issues would not in reality be able to demonstrate capacity assessment if subjected to the six tests advocated in the ruling. While Cobb made it clear these tests should only be used as guidance, there is already considerable anecdotal evidence of them being applied as *rules* when assessing an adult's capacity to engage with online services. Concerns are therefore being raised from a variety of stakeholder perspectives as to whether they are, in an increasing number of cases, leading to an unnecessary and unwarranted deprivation of liberty.

With a mix of policy, legal and at times sociological analysis, and case studies drawn from a multi-agency approach stemming from our own empirical research and experience working with practitioners, this book explores the leading edge of both policy and practice around online safeguarding for vulnerable adults with mental capacity issues. It argues that there are far more nuanced, individualised and progressive approaches for responding to online risk and safeguarding for vulnerable adults that focus on their best interests for an informed, respectful and supportive assessment.

Our work critically engages with the challenges of the tensions that arise from protectionist and participation discourses to interrogate these polarised standpoints and provide a more detailed understanding of the complexity of vulnerable adults engaging in everyday online activities and relationships. We endeavour to highlight the flawed approach and limitations of current legislative approaches and the worrying lack of knowledge in the workforce. Current practice across many sectors working with those with capacity issues has resulted in individuals having their rights to freedom of expression, privacy and access to information withdrawn based on safeguarding arguments as an excuse to excessively monitor and control individuals, which undermines their human rights (including the UN Convention of the Rights of Persons with Disabilities – UNCRPD). The book sets out *what works* for best practice in supporting vulnerable adults online, making a case for improved policy and pursuing how the Cobb ruling can be built on in an inclusive, multi-agency and individual-centric way, to argue that effective support and safeguarding online is not a one-size-fits-all approach.

Outline of the text

In Chapter 2 we outline the trajectory of online safeguarding, the development of the dominance on protecting children and young people in online spaces, and the policy thinking, such as the UK *Online Harms* White Paper, that influences policy and practice. We consider the role of statutory guidance in relation to online safeguarding of children and young people, some of the lessons learned in the last decade of academic research, and policy directions; and question how successful we have actually been in practice, from both academic and professional perspectives. The chapter explores approaches to safeguarding adults and critically considers the rhetoric of multi-agency working to outline the key debates in dominant discourses in relation to safeguarding adults online and the roles local authorities, health and social care and law enforcement, as well as non-statutory agencies, play in safeguarding practices in the UK. The chapter explores the risks associated with being online, for example grooming and exploitation (both sexual and financial) as, we know from our research, these are poorly understood.

Throughout we have sought to examine social inclusion in the current context of the fundamental rights people have to access information, to privacy, to managing aspects of their financial lives and shopping as well as social lives and relationships online and the support they need to do so whether through official, formal care roles or more informal ones such as family and friends for example. The chapter articulates the often polarised viewpoints of the positive benefits of reducing social isolation, education and learning and access to news and areas of personal interest and the negative risks from scams, unwanted sexualised and/or violent content and potential harms. We also highlight the potentially flawed safeguarding decisions made by professionals who might, with the best of intentions, put provision and practice in place that impacts negatively on individuals' rights and does little to achieve the desired safety. The chapter also begins to explore the flaws in the constant safeguarding narrative around technology being the solution to online issues, and the origins of this thinking.

We explore in the book the risks associated with these activities, such as oversharing of personal information, trusting people potentially vulnerable adults do not know outside of the online world, and private/intimate messaging and images that can arise as a result of online friendships. We know from our work that there is very little training currently available that relates realistically to adult online safeguarding, and that there is a glaring dearth of research in the area. This book combines the two to present a grounded and practical presentation of research findings in order to develop both professional practice and the body of knowledge in the area. The following paragraphs introduce the remainder of the book and provide a rationale for its structure, moving from theoretical and legal perspectives to more grounded practical approaches.

Chapter 3 covers the legal framework and legislative developments which underpin the MCA, the Care Act 2014 (UK Government, 2014) and statutory guidance which sets out responsibilities for professionals working together. Together with these key tenets of the arguments, the chapter considers how the MCA contributes to safeguarding the best interests principle in decision making for vulnerable adults in their online lives.

With a focus on the second principle of the five set out in the MCA that 'a person is not to be treated as unable to make a decision unless all practicable steps to help him do so have been taken without success' the chapter questions the notion of person-centred emancipatory practice (revisited in Chapter 8) in maximising and assessing mental capacity and the role of ethical decision making in professional practice in relation to online spaces for vulnerable adults though the Cobb J ruling in *Re A* and *Re B* and relevant Court of Protection rulings in the UK (for example [2020] EWCOP 24) and the wider UK legal system. The chapter will also explore the right to online participation by vulnerable adults drawing upon the UNCRPD and Article 8 of the European Convention on Human Rights (ECHR), making it clear that participation is a right for all and identifying value bias that professionals might bring to assessment (for example [2020] EWCOP 24).

Chapter 4 follows the analysis set out in Chapter 3 to critically examine in detail the legacy of *Re A* and *Re B* and explores rulings that have followed these rulings.

This chapter develops from the previous two by looking in more detail around current policy agendas that relate to the area of adult online safeguarding through this analysis and by examining subsequent Court of Protection rulings in detail. It demonstrates both positive and negative impacts of the *Re A* and *Re B* cases, highlighting issues in judgments that perhaps set the bar too high for those with capacity issues, how 'experts' can make claims that have little basis in fact when examined, and, perhaps most importantly, how 'the internet and social media', the now established term for capacity to engage with any online technology, is far too broad when considering capacity. In particular we highlight a recent judgment where Williams J raised this point and which moves thinking forward such that those with caring responsibilities need to argue protection from harmful practices without withdrawing positive experiences online. The chapter also explores the forthcoming Online Safety Bill,[1] argued to be the most progressive online safeguarding legislation in the world, as the leading edge of policy thinking, and demonstrates a lack of consideration for vulnerable adults or a focus on the rights of the individual. The chapter aims to provide a reflection on current dominant discourses around online safeguarding approaches and provide a legal analysis of law related to online crime, its flaws and its impact upon those with mental capacity issues and learning difficulties.

The dominant narrative in the *Online Harms* White Paper and draft Online Safety Bill and subsequent policy direction has been to isolate and categorise harms into specific behaviours and then propose approaches to either reduce or eliminate them. This chapter will argue that the essence of this approach is flawed in its isolationist approach, in both failing to understand that online behaviours may only reach a harmful threshold as a result of wider acts, and that a mitigation approach that essentially looks to block or withdraw service fails to appreciate the social dimensions of the potential for abuse. For example, if we are to take a scenario of image-based abuse, while the act (or harm) identified in the policy sphere is the non-consensual sharing of an intimate image, this act might actually take place in a broad social context of domestic abuse, which the harms agenda fails to consider.

Chapter 5 leads on from the legacy of the Cobb ruling to ask whether professionals and practitioners are in position to provide effective support to those in their care in relation to engaging with virtual environments and in assessing an individual's capacity to make decisions about their online life. As everyday interactions online comprise a milieu of activities from financial to social to exploring and interacting, effective support requires both an in-depth understanding of the individual and knowledge of the nature and arguably the risk associated with a variety of activities. This chapter draws on empirical data and professional reflections on knowledge, understanding and training in relation to online safeguarding to challenge some of the taken-for-granted assumptions made about online risk and to question the often overlooked rights to online content. It examines the changing roles of professional practice in statutory organisations and legal practice to include cyber/digital/online and critically considers curriculum developments in these areas and unhelpful but well-established narratives such as the *digital native* (see Prensky, 2001).

While the focus of the majority chapters in this book centres around online risk in relation to mental capacity, for example relating to a learning disability or following a brain injury, Chapter 6 more specifically focuses on the debate on mental health. There has been increasing concern about the widespread impact of online harms on mental health. For example, the recent data published by Report Harmful Content (RHC) (Sharratt, 2020) found that 32 per cent of clients reported negative mental health impacts as a result of viewing harmful content online, with 13 per cent reporting suicidal ideation. This chapter explores the complex relationship between mental capacity and mental health and the increasing use of pro-sites by vulnerable adults. As we argue both in this book and elsewhere (Phippen and Bond, 2021), *vulnerability* is not a static concept and while there may not be previously acknowledged mental capacity issues, mental health may have a significant impact on mental capacity. Using examples from pro-eating disorders, pro-self-harm and pro-suicide online communities and forums, this chapter examines the phenomena of 'pro-sites', their significance in understanding and managing mental health and the importance of understanding their influence with vulnerable adults. How and why people use 'pro-content' to learn about and seek acceptance and belonging in an online community and how this behaviour can prevent recovery is only recently beginning to be understood. According to Sharratt (2020) reporting of harmful content including graphic/violent content, self-harm/suicide content or violent pornography and sexualised self-harm is on the increase. It has been well recognised that vulnerable adults use such sites as they often experience a lack of acceptance and understanding in the 'real world' and find a sense of belonging and friendship online with like-minded others (Bond, 2012; 2018).

We argue that while calls to ban these sites and restrict access to such content have been ineffectual, supporting vulnerable adults to understand how and why they are using them, often alongside pro-recovery content, in a non-judgemental way can enable a more realistic understanding of their mental health, the underlying factors why they are seeking support online and how more effective support may also be sought elsewhere that offers more positive and healthier information and advice.

The final chapter before we offer our concluding thoughts in Chapter 8 brings together theoretical, legal and practice-based perspectives to consider how stakeholders with safeguarding responsibilities best respond to online risk based upon our experience of 'what works' and how vulnerable adults can have their best interests supported. This chapter builds on the arguments set out previously in Chapter 5 to further consider the role of technology such as filtering and monitoring in safeguarding, what works, how it can be empowering, and when it can be excessive. By providing a counter-narrative, the chapter returns to one of the book's central messages – that there is not a one-size-fits-all approach to the safeguarding of vulnerable adults when it comes to online behaviours, and cognisance of their capacity issues, specific online risks, and what would be appropriate risk mitigation is required. The chapter makes a strong case for up-to-date professional knowledge and a safeguarding approach constantly mindful of the best interests of the individual. However, we would reiterate that this is not a 'how to' text book or guidance document for those working with adults who might experience capacity issues around engagement with the internet and social media. A perennial challenge we have observed in our considerable experience in research and practice around online safeguarding is a view from many to 'give us a resource that will resolve all of these issues'. There really is no such thing because decisions need to be made on a case-by-case basis that is cognisant of the individual's needs and the specific online risk.

The book concludes by reflecting once more on the foundations laid by the Cobb ruling and how we are at the genesis of both thinking and practice around adult online safeguarding. In the concluding chapter we draw conclusions regarding how the essence of the MCA and best interests should be at the forefront of any safeguarding decision and that we have the opportunity to avoid the mistakes made in the child online safeguarding world, with a focus on inclusivity and empowerment (while being mindful of risk mitigation) rather than prohibition and the withdrawal of the rights of individuals under the guise of safeguarding concern.

There is, to date, very little research on this topic yet it is of increasing concern to a wide variety of professional practice in adult social care and wider service provision (for example, housing providers who provide internet access in shared accommodation or those who provide public services such as libraries) and, as such, this publication is highly topical and relevant to academics and students in law, social policy, criminology, social work, sociology, education and mental health practice, as well as for professionals in adult social care and legal professionals working in the Court of Protection area, and also the Office of the Public Guardian of the Lasting Power of Attorney (LPA). We hope that it will also spark interest and increase awareness for policy makers and commissioners working in social and disability fields, police and criminal justice professionals, healthcare professionals, civil society, advocacy groups and non-governmental organisations (NGOs).

Note
[1]   At the time of writing the Online Safety Bill is still subject to debate and in draft form. It is expected to reach assent in 2022.

2

The context of online safeguarding

Introduction

In this chapter we consider the wider context of online safeguarding. One of the fundamental arguments we put forward in this book is that a turning point in adult online safeguarding arose with the joint Court of Protection judgments in *Re A* [2019] EWCOP 2 and *Re B* [2019] EWCOP 3, and the subsequent ruling on the appeal against the *Re B* judgment [2019] EWCA Civ 913, given that Cobb J spent a lot of time in his judgment considering the nature of online safeguarding and where professionals might go to build a knowledge base around the issues their clients are facing and the MCA. We explore these judgments later in this chapter, and subsequently their legacy in more detail in Chapter 4, where we also explore their impact on the consideration of digital rights afforded to those adults with mental capacity issues.

While the concept of online safeguarding for children and young people is well explored from both research and policy perspectives, and there are many statutory requirements on stakeholders to ensure effective training and education in this area, the same cannot be said for adults with learning difficulties and mental capacity issues, and for those supporting them. Indeed, we find a dearth of academic research, policy direction or practice guidance related to these difficulties and challenges, leaving those with safeguarding responsibilities for vulnerable adults to make poorly informed judgements on their capacity to engage with online services and confusion as to how best to support them. Both of the judgments by Cobb J made it clear (and this was most certainly one of the primary motivations for this book) that there was very little evidence, support or guidance for practitioners working in the adult safeguarding arena that would be effectively applied in these cases. Therefore, Cobb J turned to the more established world of child online safeguarding for guidance and support in making these judgements, something we will explore in more detail later in this chapter.

We feel, however, given that the knowledge base around child online safeguarding so strongly informed the judgments, and they subsequently have informed other judgments, that it is worthwhile to explore the context and history of online child safeguarding, in order to more accurately understand the current landscape. It should be noted that there are many reasons, predominantly political rather than evidence led, that have resulted in the current online safeguarding landscape. Being able to understand those gives us a better understanding of the difficulties in transferring these concepts to the adult context, as well as attempts to steer thinking around adult online safeguarding away from some of the errors made in arriving at current practice in online child safeguarding, being predominantly:

- a prohibitive mindset;
- based on the belief that technology can 'solve' the social and emotional issues that arise from online interaction;
- privileging the withdrawal of individuals' rights-based issues in order that we might ensure their safety online.

Therefore, this first substantive chapter outlines the trajectory of online safeguarding and the development of the dominance of protecting children and young people in online spaces. It looks at the role of statutory guidance for online safeguarding of children and young people and explores some of the lessons learned in the last decade from academic research and policy directions and it questions how successful we have actually been in practice. We look at perspectives on safeguarding adults and critically consider the rhetoric of multi-agency working to outline the key debates in dominant discourses in online safeguarding in relation to adults and the roles local authorities, health and social care and law enforcement, as well as non-statutory agencies, play in safeguarding practices in the UK. The chapter explores the risks associated with being online, for example grooming and exploitation (both sexual and financial), as we know from our research that these are poorly understood. We explore in more detail the concept of *vulnerability* in relation to adults in Chapter 7. However, it should be acknowledged throughout this text that vulnerability should be considered a social construction rather than a medical model, and vulnerability will vary depending on disability, capacity and life course.

We examine the current context of the fundamental rights people have to access information, to privacy, to managing aspects of their financial lives and shopping as well as their social lives and relationships online and to the support they need to fulfil these rights, whether through official, formal care roles or more informal caring roles via family and friends. The chapter underpins the development of the following chapters to examine the often polarised viewpoints of the positive benefits of reducing social isolation, education and learning and access to news and areas of personal interest in contrast to the negative risks from scams, unwanted sexualised and/or violent content and potential harms.

Furthermore, we foreground the text in real-life examples of some of the complex dilemmas that professionals, carers and families have faced in confronting online risks such as financial exploitation, emotional distress, and illegal content and activity.

Learning from the child online safeguarding arena

From our perspective, the Court of Protection decisions in the *Re A (Capacity: Social Media and Internet Use: Best Interests)* [2019] EWCOP 2 and *Re B (Capacity: Social Media: Care and Contact)* [2019] EWCOP 3 judgments present some interesting reflections, given our extensive experience (collectively nearly 40 years) in the online safeguarding space, about where the criminal justice system is in relation to protecting those with mental capacity issues and how we might best support them, while, at the same time, ensuring they are safe from harm. Furthermore, it is important to remember that we should not assume that vulnerability or specific mental capacity issues mean that an individual will not have capacity to make judgements around *any* area of their life. As the MCA Code of Practice (UK Government, 2013b) states, '[a] person's capacity must be assessed specifically in terms of their capacity to make a particular decision'. Thus, we cannot assume that because an individual does not have capacity in one area of their life they do not have capacity in others. This is vitally important in considering how decisions are made in relation to online access for people with a learning disability or impaired mental capacity. As we have observed from many years of research and practice around online safeguarding, the problem with the online safety space, as we have already explored elsewhere at great length (Bond and Phippen, 2019a, Bond and Phippen, 2019b; Phippen and Bond, 2020), is that in our rush to develop quotable soundbites and simple messaging we are failing to appreciate the diversity of motivations and behaviours of people, or to treat them as individuals. And the parlance of section 1 of the MCA, where we are assuming a person has capacity unless it has been established that they lack capacity, is very much at odds with this thinking.

However, just as we argue in Chapter 6 that the draft Online Safety Bill fails to differentiate between the identified *harms*, the Cobb J rulings seem to have established, in both Court of Protection rulings and more widely across social care practice, that the *internet and social media* is a single entity rather than the underpinning technologies for a wide range of services, behaviours and actions. One does not *do* social media, one uses social media to interact with friends and family, to follow interests, to keep track of current affairs, etc. The internet is even more broad, providing the connecting technology for social media platforms, but also communication, gaming, accessing information, watching TV and movies, shopping, social connectivity for family, friends and strangers, dating and so on. While the MCA might drive thinking towards consideration for the individual rather than blanket judgements, defining *internet and social media* as a single, broad concept is a step backwards which masks both the reality and the diversity of online provision and usage. We should, instead, be considering whether an individual has capacity to use digital technology specifically for making new friends or dating, for example, or for carrying out financial transactions or accessing information or entertainment.

While we admire Cobb J, and others involved in these rulings, wishing to base their decisions upon an evidence base, as opposed to (the frequently adopted but little recognised practice of) bringing their own opinions, value biases and media-shaped thinking, we do have concerns that basing adult online safeguarding upon the more established field (both academically and legal) of child online safeguarding risks repeating the mistakes of the past.

Given the many years of research, policy decision and stakeholder practice in online safety, our own experiences show little deviation in findings from discussions with children and young people in 2005–09 (Phippen, 2009; Bond, 2010; 2013; 2014) to the present day (UK Safer Internet Centre, 2017). Given that youth discourse has not developed or matured in well over 10 years, we would, quite rightly, question whether the thinking and discourse within online child safeguarding in this time has been recognised. Surely, if things had progressed, young people would have a different perspective now?

Within the child safeguarding arena, for example, those who wish to protect remain firmly rooted in their narrow viewpoints rather than listening and educating, and policy perspectives move little beyond victim blaming, apathy and engagement with risk discourses, even though prohibitive messages have been delivered to young people for over 15 years with little meaningful impact. If we are to consider a well-researched, and debated, aspect of online child safety – teen sexting (the exchange of intimate images by teenagers) – we know from our empirical work that the key educational message was 'don't do this, it's illegal!'. Clearly, this has certainly not been effective (Phippen and Bond, 2019a)! At the time, young people were calling for education and routes for disclosure that would not risk their being criminalised. Despite online technology having a taken-for-granted, ubiquitous role in everyday relationships (Ling, 2012), including intimate relationships (Bond, 2011; 2014), in the UK government's 2019 curriculum definition of Relationships and Sex Education (DfE, 2019: 30), which finally became statutory, the only mention of teen sexting in the whole document lies in the section on *The Law*, accompanied by the rather chilling statement: 'There are also many different legal provisions whose purpose is to protect young people and which ensure young people take responsibility for their actions.'

Rather than continue to repeat and reinforce victim-blaming rhetoric, we see, and we indeed hope, that with the Cobb J judgments and the wider debate that has emerged, there is an opportunity to not make the same mistakes of child online safeguarding and over-protectionist approaches, but to take a victim-centric approach that does more than provide victims with finger wagging and shrugs. This book, therefore, aims to encourage an approach that leaves what we might refer to as *digital unconscious bias* out of professional judgements and instead introduce a perspective that considers the rights of the individual – their rights to participation, and to privacy, not just to protection – critical thinking, and a recognition of their best interests.

Re A and *Re B*

The 2019 Court of Protection judgments in *Re A* [2019] EWCOP 2 and *Re B* [2019] EWCOP 2, and the subsequent ruling in the appeal against the *Re B* judgment (EWCA, 2019), have provided much food for thought around the online safeguarding of adults with mental capacity issues. They once again raise questions on the efficacy of legislation in general for protecting victims and the public at large, and from a more academic perspective, raise questions around why the law struggles so fundamentally to effectively tackle online harms. Furthermore, it allows us to reflect on the challenges of policing online behaviour, particularly of those who are vulnerable (whether they be children and young people or adults), without detrimentally and disproportionately affecting their fundamental human rights.

While there are some aspects of the judgments that fall outside of the scope of our focus here to see the direction of travel for online adult safeguarding where the individual has mental capacity issues, there are overlaps (such as sexual consent and accommodation provision) that are meaningful to explore. However, the intention of this analysis is not to conduct a detailed exploration of the judgments, but rather to explore them in the context of the foundations upon which they were built – child online safeguarding – and to review how these rulings and the subsequent 'test' of crucial values might better progress adult online safeguarding and avoid some of the well-established but often conveniently overlooked pitfalls of the child online safeguarding space.

There is much to admire in the judgments. We can see from them that these landmark rulings acknowledge the struggle with the balance in acknowledging the individuality of each case when set against 'rules' that might be applied in subsequent cases and how *Best Interest* (as also set out in section 1 of the MCA 2005) might effectively be applied in future cases that might draw upon these judgments. The *Re A* and *Re B* judgments have, in their considered discussion and measured thinking, demonstrated that adult online safeguarding presents many challenges that are not faced in the child online safety world, particularly around the responsibilities of stakeholders or clear legislation given the lack of statutory safeguarding requirements. Or, to put it another way, without the statutory framework that exists around child online safeguarding, there is an opportunity to bring critical thinking to judgements and focus more effectively on individual need, interests and well-being.

Within the child online safeguarding arena stakeholders are bound by statutory instruments such as the *Keeping Children Safe in Education* (DfE, 2018) guidance and legislation clearly setting out protection of children (for example the Protect of Children Act 1978 (UK Government, 1978), Sexual Offences Act 2003 (UK Government, 2003) and Serious Crime Act 2015 (UK Government, 2015a), however within the adult safeguarding arena the legislation around stakeholder responsibility is less clear. The Care Act 2014 (UK Government, 2014) makes no mention of online safeguarding provision and the MCA, while empowering to those with mental capacities issues, does not attempt to define how online safeguarding might manifest (which is beyond the scope of the legislation).

Applying the 3Cs

Cobb J develops this thinking by detailing a test that could be used in future cases to consider whether an individual has capacity to make decisions on online risk, and again this is in many ways to be applauded. However, in developing a test that might be applied to future cases, we note that Cobb J refers to the UK Council for Internet Safety's *Child Safety Online: A Practical Guide for Providers of Social Media and Interactive Services* (DCMS, 2016) as a foundation for the test's development. The basis of this argument falls on the concept of the 3Cs, a long-applied tool in the child online safety space (Livingstone and Haddon, 2009):

> **Content risk**: children receiving mass-distributed content. This may expose them to age-inappropriate material such as pornography, extreme violence, or content involving hate speech and radicalization.

> **Conduct risk**: children participating in an interactive situation. This includes bullying, sexting, harassing. Being aggressive or stalking; or promoting harmful behaviour such as self-harm, suicide, pro-anorexia, bulimia, illegal drug use or imitating dangerous behaviour. A child's own conduct online can also make them vulnerable- for example, by over-sharing their personal information or by harassing or bullying themselves.

> **Contact risk**: children being victims of interactive situations. This includes being bullied, harassed or stalked; meeting strangers; threats to privacy, identity and reputation (for example through embarrassing photos shared without permission, a house location being identified, someone impersonating a user, users sharing information with strangers); and violence, threats and abuse directly aimed at individual users and/or groups of users.

These definitions have long been adopted (and indeed further updated) in the online child safeguarding world. They are, on occasion, a useful tool to begin a discussion around online risk for young people. Indeed, they broadly categorise the nature of online risks, to a certain degree. However, as we have already stated, building the foundations for vulnerable adult online safeguarding on child-centric approaches is not without its problems nor its tensions. We argue that the 3Cs is a simplistic model that assumes a passivity of child and the victim-centricity of approach. The dominant discourses in the social construction of childhood depicting the child as innocent and in need of protecting (Jenks, 2005), assumes that the actor of these behaviours, whether content, conduct or contact, will be a victim of abuse or harm, rather than a perpetrator. While the Conduct aspect of the rules implies a more active role by the child in an online scenario, it still views this from a position of placing oneself in a position of vulnerability as a result, not that they might be the instigator of abuse, and the actor causing the harm. However, there is a considerable body of research which evidences that *the child* is both victim and threat (Gittens, 1998; James et al, 2010) literally and metaphorically. As we have already suggested, the legislative framework for adult safeguarding is far less well defined and, in the event of the subject of care being found to be offending, the legislation is less likely to protect them from prosecution. There are exceptions to this, such as the exchange of intimate images, where the law for adults protects victims of non-consensual sharing, whereas there is a risk for minors in that, because the law that 'protects' them – the Protection of Children Act 1978 (UK Government, 1978) – makes no provision for the subject of an image to also be the sender of an image and the distributor of an image (Phippen and Brennan, 2020). However, in general, it is more likely that a vulnerable adult will be pursued for arrest or charge in the event of an online harm than a child.

Interestingly, Cobb J raised the complexity and uncertainty of online law in his judgment in *Re A*:

> 7. There is acknowledged public uncertainty of the law surrounding online abuse; although criminal offences do cover illegal online activity, it is acknowledged that the legislation as a whole requires clarifying, consolidating and/or rationalising in order to be more effective. It is notable in this regard that while it is a crime to incite hatred because of religion or race, it is not presently a crime to incite hatred because of disability. Those who press for a change in the legislation in this regard have a compelling case.

Therefore, while we might view the 3Cs as a useful starting point to develop understanding around what online risk might be, it fails to acknowledge the nuance and individuality of any given 'online risk' scenario and, arguably, results in attempts to disregard such complexity in our efforts to fit a risk into its appropriate 'C'. It reflects a wider wish, explored later, in the online harms policy area, for easy answers to complex situations. A young person taking an intimate image of themselves, sharing it with a consenting partner, who then shares it, non-consensually, to peers, is complex. The dominant westernised view of childhood as non-sexual (James et al, 2010) and the consistent policy position of 'don't do it, its illegal' has clearly failed a whole generation of young people because it blindly follows a piece of legislation that is no longer fit for purpose and a prohibitive mindset that hopes its unquestioning adherence to this law will stop young people doing something that as a society we would rather they did not, rather than accepting that this is something young people do as part of their everyday intimate relationships, as victims of non-consensual sharing who deserve as much protection as adults do in a similar situation.

We can see this mindset tending towards prohibitive approaches applied to other issues of complexity, where the morality of the prohibition is easier to justify in a child safeguarding environment than an adult one. For example, let us take a perennial moral quandary – online pornography. If we take this from a child-centric safeguarding perspective, we have a simple message – 'this child is accessing pornography, therefore let's filter their internet access to prevent this'. While this is the subject of much debate, especially around the fluctuating age verification legislation (UK Government, 2017) as a *solution* to this social ill, it is difficult to argue that a child *should* have access to pornography. Yet is well established that children access sexual content for information, sexual gratification and acceptance in social groups (Bond, 2014; Setty, 2020). And, as will be discussed later, there are complexities in the prohibitive approaches to child access to pornography (in that, in general, they do not work!). It becomes a far more complex rights-based issue if we consider this for an adult wishing to access pornography, which is their right as long as the content they are accessing is not extreme pornography or child abuse material. While we might take a perspective that we would rather an adult with learning difficulties does not access pornography, if we take a subjective view based upon our own value biases, it is a far more difficult think to rationalise as 'we'd rather they didn't' and it certainly would be difficult to demonstrate that this is in the best interests of the individual. This is acknowledged by Cobb J in his judgments.

Digital unconscious bias

As we have stated already, we draw extensively upon our own empirical work in this area. We do, as a result of our work, spend a great deal of time working with both those for whom the need to safeguard has been identified, and also with many stakeholders in that safeguarding arena. As such we are often placed in situations of debate around balancing the wish to keep an individual safe from the risk of harm with their rights to experience life to the fullest and, as such, being allowed to engage with the risks in order to also recognise, understand and learn to manage risk. We present in the following text three scenarios that have arisen within our work. The first was a conversation with a social care team who had responsibility for the care of a young adult male with mental capacity issues related to autistic spectrum disorder. This conversation went some way to highlight that the lack of knowledge of online safeguarding, or clear guidance to those stakeholders with safeguarding responsibility, result in some truly concerning responses that fit squarely into what we have referred to elsewhere as the *safeguarding dystopia* (Phippen, 2016).

In this case the social care team were recounting the challenges of caring for this young man, who was living independently, but the team had concerns regarding both his use of online technologies and also the risk of harm arising from independent living. Their *solution* (for it is a solution only in the broadest definition of the term) was to place a series of online cameras around the young man's home so they could monitor him remotely while, they perceived, 'allowing' him his independence. "The trouble is," we were told by one of the team, "we keep on seeing him masturbate." Not only is this illustrative of Rogers' (2016) observation that sexual pleasure for intellectually disabled people is often mediated through surveillance and governance and societal attitudes to disability and sexuality more generally, but also a very clear, uncomfortable, demonstration of how, in the emergent age of casual surveillance of society (see Lyon, 2001), technical solutions with little care for an individual's privacy can also be applied to vulnerable adults. In order to ensure this young man was 'safe' those stakeholders with safeguarding responsibilities decided the only solution was to strip him of any right to privacy and provide an approach that was clearly not in the best interests of their client. However, they did perceive that the erosion of the young man's rights was justifiable to make sure he was not at risk. A phrase we often hear is 'safeguarding is more important than privacy'. The perspective seems to be that as long as the erosion of rights comes from a good place, it cannot be a negative thing. Moreover, it was only because of their own discomfort in watching their client masturbate that they wished for guidance on how they might tackle this situation. Suffice to say we suggested that the surveillance was excessive, failed to address the client's best interests and should be removed. We suggested instead that regular conversations with the young man about his online activities, alongside an education programme and routes for reporting, might be a more appropriate approach.

In a different case we were asked to advise on a safeguarding concern for a vulnerable adult male who had a care team around him who were concerned he was visiting the local library to access (legal) pornography.

His condition meant he had trouble understanding that the public viewing of pornography was unacceptable or might make others feel uncomfortable. The care team's view was that this was (unsurprisingly) unacceptable and he was upsetting other library users and they wanted to know how they might prevent their client accessing pornography. The library, unsurprisingly, was proposing banning him from the setting unless he stopped accessing pornography there.

We did query why he had to go to the library to access online information and content, and whether this was the only means for him to go online. We were told he did have a laptop but it was "full of viruses" and was not workable. When asked why they had not had the laptop fixed, it was the view of the care team that if they did that, he would be able to access pornography on it. At no point did the care team provide a rationale as to why this adult male might have a condition that meant accessing pornography would be harmful to him, they just wanted to stop him doing it. The main concern of the care team was that the gentleman should be prevented from accessing pornography, even though there was nothing to suggest that what he was looking at was illegal or there was any professional view that viewing legal pornography would have a negative impact upon his well-being. The view was expressed that perhaps preventing the gentleman from accessing pornography was, of itself, a contravention of his human rights, and the focus of concern should lie with rectifying the issues with his laptop and install anti-virus software so he was not compelled to try to access pornography when he visited the library. We also observed that the library was within its rights to prevent access to certain types of content on their public network, but the gentleman himself should not be prevented from *any* access to legal content just because the care team found it unpalatable. Furthermore, banning him from the library also meant preventing him from reading the comic books and magazines he enjoyed reading and could not afford to buy and from talking to some of the regular library staff and others with whom he liked to chat.

Our final example case is drawn from one we encountered when delivering training to early career social care professionals, namely a concerned individual who was uncomfortable with what he saw during his first work placement. He told us that he worked in a residential setting for adults with learning difficulties. The senior managers in the setting were concerned about the potential harm that could arise from residents using digital technology, and one had been the subject of financial extortion as a result of an online scam. The management solution was therefore to instigate a 'spot-checking' regime within the setting, so staff would conduct checks on the devices of residents, supposedly whenever they wished to although in reality it was more likely to take place at scheduled times of day, to ensure they were engaging with online services free of harm and risk.

We should stress that all of the residents of the setting were adults, and none were subject to any Court of Protection rulings that had indicated that they did not have capacity to engage with online content and services. When the professional we were discussing this case with raised concerns about the potential breaches of privacy (and potential data protection risks) associated with this practice, they were told that it was acceptable because all residents had *consented* to these checks and, besides, 'safeguarding trumps privacy rights'. Perhaps the most uncomfortable thing about this practice was the belief that consent had been received, given some of the learning difficulties experienced by some residents, and the fact they essentially had little choice – what would have happened if one of the residents had not consented? Or perhaps the organisation is confusing consent with assent?

In each of these cases we see a clear demonstration of:

- a failure to appreciate the rights of the vulnerable adult;
- a view that technology can solve any safeguarding concerns;
- taking an approach where perceived solutions are in the best interest of the care team, rather than the vulnerable individual.

Clearly these brief case examples demonstrate the need for guidance for organisations and for those working with adults with mental capacity issues about how they best support clients while ensuring their rights are protected and the care provided is in their best interests. We discuss how to best support clients while protecting their rights in more detail in Chapter 7 but note here that these examples are why Cobb J's joint ruling in *Re A* and *Re B* is welcome. What is also clear from our analysis of the judgment(s) is that if we are to consider the issues for a single individual in detail, it can be extremely complex and require a careful balance between the rights of the individual, care of that person, the need to safeguard both them and potentially others, as well as any legislative position. Therefore, this is not something that can be applied to the population as a whole with an algorithm or a universal prohibitive approach. However, this sometimes flies in the face of those working in a safeguarding capacity who are looking for clear and easily applied rules in all contexts.

We also acknowledge and draw attention to the fact that the concept of safety in the online safeguarding world is a strange one, and while we will undoubtedly refer to 'online safety' throughout this text when discussing practice and policy, it is not a term with which we are comfortable. This is because while other safety paradigms are well established, and we can see how the language of safety has transferred too readily to the online world, it is in reality somewhat problematic. If we take, for example, road safety, we can see clear operational solutions to these issues: impose laws of road users, coupled with significant sanctions should they wish to flout them; an established environment (for example using standard road markings and signage) that is consistent across the legal jurisdiction; and simple education and training programmes to help those who might be considered vulnerable (for example, children and young people) to navigate this environment effectively. We can draw from the seminal work of technology lawyer and academic Lawrence Lessig in understanding why these approaches are effective in the physical space but are less effective in the digital environment. Lessig (2006: 5) laid out a very clear, albeit challenging, argument around efforts to regulate the online world, arguing that controlling behaviour online is not possible due to the nature of the environment in which the behaviour took place: 'The claim for cyberspace was not just that government would not regulate cyberspace – it was that government could not regulate cyberspace. Cyberspace was, by nature, unavoidably free. Governments could threaten, but behavior could not be controlled; laws could be passed, but they would have no real effect.' Lessig (2006) argues that in order for a regulatory environment to be a success, there were four key *modalities* (Table 2.1).

We lightly draw on Actor Network Theory (ANT) here (see Latour, 1994) to describe how all of these modalities have a significant role to play in managing and regulating a particular aspect of society, for the benefit of all. The applicability of ANT models to the practical understanding of what otherwise would seem a heterogeneous collection of materials (see Strathern, 1999) is pertinent here as within the physical world these modalities work because they are clear and adhere to natural law (physics, biology, acceptable moralities); and legislation works because it can be applied to a physical space (that is, a country, a community, a road network) without ambiguity. We have already described road safety using these modalities yet if we try to do the same for an online environment we are faced with significant challenges. Within the online world the *architecture* that exists is *code*, the raw material of digital technology (while we acknowledge that digital technology also relies on hardware – communication networks and physical devices – they are essentially non-functioning collections of wires and rare earth metals without the code to make anything happen) and the hardware upon which the code communicates. Code is designed, written and shaped by those with the skills, knowledge and talent to be able to turn the requirements of users into functional algorithms and assemble them into software platforms. These software platforms form environments

Table 2.1: Four key modalities

1. Laws	2. Social norms
3. Market	4. Architecture

Source: Authors, based on Lessig, 2006

for people to interact in various forms, whether they be social or business, and as a result of these interactions, risks arise (for example when one member of an online social community becomes abusive to another). Thus, through an ANT lens, the network is comprised of heterogeneous *actants* – human, social and technical (Latour, 1999). Thus the platforms and code, can put countermeasures in place to mitigate the risk of the abuse taking place, such as providing the potential victim with tools to be able to block and report the abuser, the code cannot, of itself, prevent the actual behaviour of the individual (human).

Lessig's primary idea is that code becomes, in essence, the law of the online world because it is the only way *rules* can be implemented. Hutchby's (2001a) concept of *affordances* is also helpful here in that there are boundaries to what code can achieve, constrained by logic and the implementation of biases of those who implement it. Code cannot implement ambiguity, imprecision or morality. It cannot only make a judgement on the behaviour of an individual based upon the data it has been presented with, and that judgement cannot be subjective. Regardless of the current excitement around the potential of artificial intelligence (something we will explore in more detail in Chapter 5), there is nothing intelligent about what these algorithms do, they simply follow rules and data, and imply intelligent decision as a result. It, or more accurately, coders, can only implement things that can be defined in a logical manner, and this presents significant challenges when tackling social issues, where system boundaries can be infinite and behaviour is unpredictable.

Returning to online safety, we can argue strongly that we cannot hope to keep people safe online in the same way we try to in a road safety context. If we start from a position of guaranteeing safety online, we are doomed to fail. We can, however, help those who engage with online platforms understand the risks associated with this engagement, and provide them with the information, knowledge and tools to mitigate those risks. The tools might be part of the architecture – the aforementioned reporting and blocking tools – or they might form some kind of education initiatives. However, we would also argue, and will present an analysis of this in this chapter, that the policy position around child online safeguarding has been one of *ensuring* safety for the last 10 years, and that has brought us to a position where there is a belief that risk should not be mitigated but eliminated. This, in turn, results in use ending up with strange and unusual safeguarding judgements and a goal that can never be achieved.

How did we get here?

Governments of the Industrial World, you weary giants of flesh and steel, I come from Cyberspace, the new home of Mind. On behalf of the future, I ask you of the past to leave us alone. You are not welcome among us. You have no sovereignty where we gather.

This quotation is taken from John Perry Barlow's (1996) *Declaration of Independence for Cyberspace*, a much-cited manifesto that claimed governments would always fail to control the online world. The declaration was written on the day the US Telecommunications Act 1996 (FFC, 1996) came into force. While the US government claimed this Act would introduce great competition to the telecommunications infrastructure market, those who opposed it claimed it would consolidate power into the hands of a few major corporations (which turned out to be true). Internet libertarians, who wished for a free and neutral digital world, felt these early attempts to control online communications and place it in a competitive space were doomed to fail. The declaration continues: 'Cyberspace does not lie within your borders. Do not think that you can build it, as though it were a public construction project. You cannot. It is an act of nature and it grows itself through our collective actions.' Yet, over 20 years after this declaration, we see increasing attempts to regulate the online world – applying geographically distinct legislation to a global phenomenon that evolved and emerged through convergence and mutual interest, rather than commercial interests and market forces. Commerce and governments only discovered the internet once it was established and therefore had little chance to exploit it or regulate it as it grew. This declaration does bring attention to an interesting tension between online technology and the need for governments to govern and pass legislation that protects citizens from potential harms and regulates their antisocial behaviour. We would not take exception to this. The Declaration of Independence for Cyberspace is not so much a claim that *anything* that happens online cannot be regulated, more that trying to legislate to change the infrastructure and technology of the online environment will neither achieve its aims nor be effective legislation. We have already discussed earlier how Lessig's perspectives on technology regulation support this position – if one cannot control the modalities of regulation, or if some of those modalities do not even exist, regulation is doomed to fail.

Understandably, governments wish to mitigate risk and reduce harm for those going online, and to ensure they are *safe*, and this desire to ameliorate risk and harm impacts on organisations providing care, services and support to vulnerable individuals. We are supportive of this position. We are not proposing a position where anyone should be allowed to do anything online without risk of punishment. There are, in the more unpleasant areas of social media, many people who believe freedom of speech means they should be able to say anything they wish (Howard, 2019). However, they fail to grasp that freedom of speech does not mean freedom from consequences. If, as a result of their wish to express themselves freely, they end up projecting hateful communication, it is right that they should be punished for this. However, we are also sufficiently experienced and knowledgeable in the online safeguarding area to know that regulation that fails to understand the underpinning technologies, or believe that these same technologies can tackle what are, in essence, social problems, is doomed to fail.

There is a famous cybersecurity practitioner, Marcus Ranum (Cheswick et al, 2003), who is much quoted as saying '[y]ou can't solve social problems with software'. Sometimes referred to as Ranum's Law, this is something with which we would wholeheartedly agree, and something we will explore later in this chapter and in more detail in Chapter 5.

Arguably, the drive to keep citizens 'safe' online, particularly from a policy/legal perspective, has, at its core, arisen from a wish to prevent children from accessing pornography. All that has followed in the policy area began with discussions that formed in the UK with an All-Party Inquiry into Child Online Safety in 2012 (Independent Parliamentary Inquiry into Online Child Protection, 2012), which was the catalyst for a speech made in 2013 by the then British Prime Minister David Cameron (UK Government, 2013a). In this speech Mr Cameron stated:

> I want to talk about the internet, the impact it's having on the innocence of our children, how online pornography is corroding childhood and how, in the darkest corners of the internet, there are things going on that are a direct danger to our children and that must be stamped out.

Mr Cameron continued with proposals on how to tackle each problem – two issues we would argue are very different, regardless of the proposals that seemed to suggest a similar approach to both. First, concerning tackling child abuse images online:

> You're the people who have worked out how to map almost every inch of the earth from space who have developed algorithms that make sense of vast quantities of information. You're the people who take pride in doing what they say can't be done. You hold hackathons for people to solve impossible internet conundrums. Well – hold a hackathon for child safety. Set your greatest brains to work on this. You are not separate from our society, you are part of our society, and you must play a responsible role in it.

Clearly, access to child abuse imagery is a challenge online and one where there are very clear legal definitions. This is illegal content, unquestionably. However, Mr Cameron also refers to tackling youth access to online pornography:

By the end of this year, when someone sets up a new broadband account the settings to install family friendly filters will be automatically selected. If you just click 'next' or 'enter', then the filters are automatically on. And, in a really big step forward, all the ISPs [Internet Service Providers] have rewired their technology so that once your filters are installed, they will cover any device connected to your home internet account. No more hassle of downloading filters for every device, just one click protection. One click to protect your whole home and keep your children safe.

This is a far less clear scenario legally speaking. There is nothing illegal in a child accessing pornography, but it is a behaviour where there is a view (and one we would not disagree with) that children accessing pornography can be harmful. However, Mr Cameron, by combining the two very difficult types of content access in the same speech, seems to propose they are similar in terms of approach to prevent access.

This direction focused upon the use of technology to solve issues related to online child protection and safeguarding. The view was that given the online environment presents *risks* or *harms* (for example, access to inappropriate content such as pornography, access to harmful content that might relate to images of self-harm and suicide, abuse via messaging and chat platforms or the sharing of a self-generated indecent image of a minor) that might ultimately harm the child in some manner, the technology must also be able to provide the solution to prevent these things from happening (a point we explore further in Chapter 6). The focus in the early foundations of this policy direction was the prevention of access to pornographic content by children and young people. The solution was seen to be filtering technologies, which would identify pornographic materials and prevent access.

Digital technology is certainly very good at clearly defined, rule-based functionality in easily contained system boundaries; or, to put it another way, data processing, analysis and pattern matching of data – looking for things they know about and finding them in big unwieldy systems. Computers are very good at taking data and analysing it based upon rules defined within the system (for example, identifying words that *might* relate to sexual content). However, they are far less good at is interpretation, *intelligence* and inference. What computers cannot do is something they have not been instructed to do. Everything they do has to be defined in code, which requires it to be defined in a manner that cannot be subject to interpretation.

By way of an illustrative, albeit mischievous but useful, example, let us consider the word 'cock'. This is a term that *might* be related to a sexual context – it could refer to male genitalia. Equally, it might refer to a male bird. If we consider this from the perspective of a filtering system that might be tasked with ensuring an end user cannot access websites of a sexual nature, we might provide that system with a list of keywords that could indicate sexual content. 'Cock' may be one of these terms. The filtering system will be very good at pattern matching this string of characters to any mentioned within any given website and will successfully block access to this content. However, it will be far less good at determining the actual context of the website – it *might* be about sexual activity; however, it might also be about poultry or livestock.

Even with this simple example, we can see how it might struggle to prevent access to all sexual content or, equally, result in false positives – blocking innocuous sites. We use the term *innocuous* sites to describe those that have been incorrectly blocked based upon the requirements of the filter, for example pornography, gambling, drugs and alcohol, and not the term *legal*, because access to pornography is legal in the UK and to describe sites that are not 'inappropriate' for children to see (also referred to as overblocking). Given the policy direction, and the pressure exacted upon service providers as a result, it is likely that algorithms will be implemented to be conservative in their filtering – worrying less about overblocking and more at ensuring as much sexual content as possible is captured. A simple and popular example of this comes from the overblocking of the northern English town of Scunthorpe (Wikipedia, online), given that a substring of its composition is a vulgar word for female genitalia.

From a human rights perspective, these proactive filtering approaches have already attracted the concern of the United Nations, with the *Report of the Special Rapporteur on the promotion and protection of the right to freedom of opinion and expression* (UNHRC, 2018) stating that '[s]tates and intergovernmental organizations should refrain from establishing laws or arrangements that would require the "proactive" monitoring or filtering of content, which is both inconsistent with the right to privacy and likely to amount to pre-publication censorship'. Nevertheless, there seems to be an increased focus on interceptional content moderation from platform providers, and an expectation to monitor behaviour on these platforms in a more proactive manner (with automated intervention), with the threat of legislation should these calls not be heeded. This is a policy focus that began with young people's access to pornography, and the unacceptability of this, but the policy legacy has continued to demand the technical solution to tackle any form of online safeguarding.

This can be clearly seen in the fluctuating age verification debate in the UK (at the time of writing, it seems the UK government, and some European governments, have decided that this is a good way to prevent access to pornography again (Politico, 2021)). Legislation was established in the UK in the Digital Economy Act 2017 Part 3 (UK Government, 2017), which mandated providers whose services provide commercial access to pornography to implement age verification technology such as to ensure no UK citizen under the age of 18 could access their content. To take this seemingly simple example, let us consider how we might prevent children from accessing pornography. From a logical perspective, there are two main requirements in order to achieve this:

- we know the age of the end user;
- we know that a piece of content is pornographic.

If we can achieve this, we can prevent children from accessing such content. However, if we take each point in turn:

- Unless we have some means for all citizens to be able to demonstrate their age in a digital form how do we know their age? There is not a universal, statutory identity token that exists in the UK that everyone can use to demonstrate their age.
- Can we define, in logic, what makes a piece of content pornographic if we cannot even define it in law? While attempts to define in law do exist these are of themselves ambiguous and the subject of much case law. Case law exists because the law is complex and requires debate and discussion by intelligent people to interpret the legislation and build, on a case-by-case basis, knowledge around the legislation's application to a society. However, in this case, there is an expectation that an algorithm can determine whether one of a potentially massive volume of online content contains pornographic material.

Reidenberg's (1997) work on the *Lex Informatica* very clearly pointed out the need for this understanding. He argued that digital technology imposes its own rules on how data is communicated, and what is possible in this management:

> The pursuit of technological rules that embody flexibility for information flows maximizes public policy options; at the same time, the ability to embed an immutable rule in system architecture allows for the preservation of public-order values. These tools can lessen a number of problems that traditional legal solutions face in regulating the Information Society. Yet a shift in public policy planning must occur in order for Lex Informatica to develop as an effective source of information policy rules. The new institutions and mechanisms will not be those of traditional government regulation. Policymakers must begin to look to Lex Informatica to effectively formulate information policy rules.

Put simply, as we outlined earlier, code is good at some things and poor at others, and the public policy space needs to understand where these strengths and weaknesses lie in order to make effective legislation to tackle social issues. Most importantly, they need to understand that code cannot solve *everything*. By the end of 2013 the UK government had forged an agreement with the largest four ISPs in the UK, under which the ISPs committed to offering all new customers a network-level filtering service, in the face of a threat to ISPs that if they did not do something voluntarily, the government would legislate.

The focus of responsibility lay with industry, and the threat of legislation loomed if they did not do what they were asked. Therefore, by 2013 all major ISPs had provided a suite of filtering solutions to households to ensure that children could not access pornography on home devices. After considerable government pressure, new subscribers had a default 'opt-in' to these services – when they establish a new connection the filters are switched on, and the subscriber has to make an active choice to switch them off. Existing subscribers were given the choice to install filters. This voluntary response to policy pressure was put in place in 2013 so at the time of writing has been available to subscribers for over five years. OFCOM's Media Literacy report of 2019 (OFCOM, 2019) reported a figure of 36 per cent of parents of 8–11 year olds installing filters. After five years of media reporting, service provider and government nudge, and policy drive, filters were still not used being used in the majority of the homes in the UK. The same report stated that over-blocking was rarely a reason for parents not to install filters (the most popular reason being they preferred to establish their own rules in the home for addressing internet access). This does raise the question: if these technologies are effective, why would parents not want to install them in the home?

Within this first wave of pornography prevention solutions we also saw the introduction of family-friendly WiFi (Friendly Wifi, online) in order that public WiFi access in the UK was filtered to prevent access to Child Sexual Exploitation and Abuse Material (CSAM/CSEM) and pornography (and other 'inappropriate' content):

> Simply tell us what type of websites you want to block – Adult Content, Illegal Content, Streaming Media, Chat & Instant Messaging, Social Networking, etc. – and we'll do the rest.
>
> Our proprietary internet filtering algorithms intelligently categorize sites so you don't have to constantly maintain a list of blocked sites.

Again, the differentiation of the legal and illegal is a complex one to marry into the same service and, we might reflect, probably should not be offered in one solution. Running the Internet Watch Foundation (IWF) URL list (online) means that illegal content related to CSEM can be effectively managed and it is unlikely that even the most freedom-craving internet libertarian would argue that this material should be accessible in a café WiFi hotspot. However, other forms of content blocking become more problematic and face similar problems of over-blocking.

While the introduction of Family Friend WiFi, and the resultant impact of this on other providers (that is, they also began to filter on public WiFi) (UK Safer Internet Centre, 2015), was viewed as an online safeguarding success. Perhaps with some reflection, however, this might not be as significant an achievement as it was hailed to be. Admittedly, filters continued to improve, but mainly as a result of more websites becoming *whitelisted* – where websites that were incorrectly blocked could file a report with filtering providers to add them to a list which would mean that even if the filtering algorithm detects a reason to block (for example, sexual keywords in the URL or website content), the white list will override this decision and allow the site access. This, of itself, seems a curious process. For example, a business, NGO or individual establishing a website to provide some form of service which then, due to the filtering algorithms, could end up being blocked on either public WiFi provision or home filtering (both use similar technology and in a number of cases share the same lists). The provider therefore needs to make a report to each filtering company to ask for their (entirely legal and in no way controversial) web content to be whitelisted, and then a human moderator will investigate it and if they decide it is indeed not harmful the website would be added to the whitelist.

Moreover, there is a more fundamental issue, and that is does filtering public WiFi actually solve a real problem? While it is unquestionable that any internet service provision should prevent access to illegal content, and this is why the IWF services are so well regarded and successful, is the goal of preventing children accessing pornography in cafes, libraries and supermarkets a problem we needed to tackle? There is a twofold 'protection' measure here – first, to prevent children from accessing pornography online, and secondly to prevent children seeing an adult accessing pornography online. We have posed this question many times at conferences and training events, with many stakeholders in safeguarding, and we always come to the same conclusion – we do not see individuals in public places using public WiFi to access pornography. While it would be difficult to argue that people *should* be allowed to access pornography in public space, we would suggest that all should be entitled to access sites related to sex education, gender and human rights, mental health services or any number of other innocuous sites on an internet connection. Yet family-friendly WiFI remains something that is viewed as a step forward in algorithmic child safeguarding, even if there is little evidence that the problem it is tackling actually exists.

In April 2019 the UK government released its *Online Harms* White Paper (UK Government, 2019):

> The government wants the UK to be the safest place in the world to go online, and the best place to start and grow a digital business. Given the prevalence of illegal and harmful content online, and the level of public concern about online harms, not just in the UK but worldwide, we believe that the digital economy urgently needs a new regulatory framework to improve our citizens' safety online.
>
> Illegal and unacceptable content and activity is widespread online, and UK users are concerned about what they see and experience on the internet. The prevalence of the most serious illegal content and activity, which threatens our national security or the physical safety of children, is unacceptable. Online platforms can be a tool for abuse and bullying, and they can be used to undermine our democratic values and debate. The impact of harmful content and activity can be particularly damaging for children, and there are growing concerns about the potential impact on their mental health and wellbeing.

It continued:

> This White Paper sets out a programme of action to tackle content or activity that harms individual users, particularly children, or threatens our way of life in the UK, either by undermining national security, or by undermining our shared rights, responsibilities and opportunities to foster integration.
>
> There is currently a range of regulatory and voluntary initiatives aimed at addressing these problems, but these have not gone far or fast enough, or been consistent enough between different companies, to keep UK users safe online.
>
> The UK will be the first to do this, leading international efforts by setting a coherent, proportionate and effective approach that reflects our commitment to a free, open and secure internet.
>
> As a world-leader in emerging technologies and innovative regulation, the UK is well placed to seize these opportunities. We want technology itself to be part of the solution, and we propose measures to boost the tech-safety sector in the UK, as well as measures to help users manage their safety online.
>
> The UK has established a reputation for global leadership in advancing shared efforts to improve online safety. Tackling harmful content and activity online is one part of the UK's wider ambition to develop rules and norms for the internet, including protecting

personal data, supporting competition in digital markets and promoting responsible digital design.

Perhaps the most telling comment from the opening pages of the White Paper, however, comes from the ministerial introduction, which stated the paper formed part of the 'UK's wider ambition to develop rules and norms for the internet'. Harking back to John Perry Barlow's manifesto, is it really the UK government's place to develop rules and norms for the internet? Of course, we would expect them to provide the legislation to manage behaviours that might be facilitated online that affect their citizens, but they surely cannot define *norms* for a global technology platform?

The reason we explore it here is because we can see, from David Cameron's speech, the *Online Harms* White Paper and the draft Online Safety Bill, that the focus remains one where technology needs to provide the solutions to these *technological problems*. And in the adult safeguarding examples we presented earlier in this chapter, we can see, again, how technology is viewed as the potential solution to supporting those at potential risk of harm online. As this ideology has progressed, we see many examples of *technological determinism* (see Matthewman, 2011) in the view that technology could tackle all manner of online social issues, centring around technology companies providing solutions to ensure children are safe from the variety of risks associated with going online. For example, in recent years we have had a number of calls, such as:

- a senior government minister calling for algorithms to be installed on children's mobile phones to detect indecent images and prevent them from being sent (House of Common Science and Technology Committee, 2017) (it should be noted that this statement is actually a useful proposal with which to deconstruct arguments around image recognition being used for the automatic detection of indecent images and therefore is discussed in far greater detail in Chapter 5);
- legislation to impose age verification technology on anyone wishing to access pornography from a UK-based device (House of Commons Science and Technology Committee, 2017);
- calls to extend age verification to social media sites to ensure no one under 13 can access these services and for social media companies to ensure children cannot access their services for more than two hours per day (Helm and Rawnsely, 2018);
- calls for social media companies to stop the live streaming of terrorist activities (BBC News, 2019b);
- calls for social media companies to prevent the posting of 'anti-vax' materials (Mohdin, 2019).

Yet for those of us with a knowledge of the capabilities of code, we have known for a long time that technology can only ever be a tool to support to broader social context rather than as a solution in itself to these issues. Again the concept of *affordances* and Hutchby (2001b) is helpful to our thinking here. There are some things that digital technology is very good at in this area:

- reporting routes and responsive, and transparent, take downs;
- warnings around content based upon keyword analysis and image comparison;
- pre-screening of some content that is easily identifiable as it has been previously identified as harmful or upsetting;
- monitoring network access and raising alerts using rule-based systems, for example on a known website that provides access to harmful content;
- the means to block abusers;
- interpreting new data based upon its similarity to previous data it has been shown.

However, there are other things that technology is far less good at:

- inference of context of textual content;
- identification of content outside of clearly defined heuristics;
- image processing in a broad and subjective context (for example 'indecency');
- subjective interpretation of meaning and nuance in textual data.

The culmination of this policy direction has been the publication of the draft Online Safety Bill 2021 (UK Government, 2021a) This was hailed by Oliver Dowden, Secretary of State for Culture, Media, Sport and Digital, who said (UK Government, 2021b):

> Today the UK shows global leadership with our ground-breaking laws to usher in a new age of accountability for tech and bring fairness and accountability to the online world.
> We will protect children on the internet, crack down on racist abuse on social media and through new measures to safeguard our liberties, create a truly democratic digital age.

The Home Secretary, Priti Patel, in the same press release, said:

> This new legislation will force tech companies to report online child abuse on their platforms, giving our law enforcement agencies the evidence they need to bring these offenders to justice.

Ruthless criminals who defraud millions of people and sick individuals who exploit the most vulnerable in our society cannot be allowed to operate unimpeded, and we are unapologetic in going after them.

It's time for tech companies to be held to account and to protect the British people from harm. If they fail to do so, they will face penalties.

The focus remains one of expecting those providing online services to ensure safety within them, an assumption that technology can provide the answer and if the providers do not, they will be held accountable. While, at the time of writing, the Bill is in draft form, and it would not be a useful exercise to have a detailed exploration of a piece of legislation that is, as stated by the Home Secretary, more about the accountability of technology companies than a broad piece of safeguarding legislation, it is worth reflecting upon this continuing the trajectory of technology solutions to technologically facilitated issues. It defines a wide-ranging set of powers for a regulator (OFCOM) over technology providers, to expect them to show evidence of risk assessments to demonstrate they have thought about the potential harms that might manifest on their platforms, expecting providers to implement 'safety' technologies such as monitoring and age verification, defining responsibility of platforms to manage illegal content that might be posted, but also what is defined as *legal but harmful* in the eyes of the regulator. Furthermore, it provides the government with powers to prevent app stores from carrying services that do not comply with the law, and to control access to ancillary services such as payment providers and advertisers.

The efficacy, or even implementability, of this legislation remains to be seen and could fill a separate text. For the purposes of this book, however, we will make one further observation. Within the 145 pages of the Draft Online Safety Bill there is far less mention of education, which is only referred to twice, in a section related to public awareness campaigns by the regulator. The responsibility of the service providers to *do more* and to expect technological solutions to what are essentially technologically facilitated social problems is rife in the online safeguarding space and can frequently cause tension between the technology providers and the policy makers. One of the fundamental points we make no apology for repeating is that technology cannot be the solution to online safeguarding.

As we have already discussed, there is a risk in our rush to safeguard and protect everyone from the 'darkest corners of the internet' that we adopt approaches that do not consider individuals' rights and, in some cases, erode them. There is no piece of legislation that says that safeguarding trumps privacy. The Data Protection Act 2018 (UK Government, 2018) lays down some provision for safeguarding exceptions (in Schedule 8 of the legislation) but they are limited and still very mindful of individuals' data protection rights. We would argue that there is a lack of understanding *in* the stakeholder space because there is a lack of understanding *of* the stakeholder space itself (Phippen and Bond, 2019a). We defined a stakeholder model for online child protection (Bond and Phippen, 2019b), which is reproduced in Figure 2.1, and which is of itself an adaptation of the seminal work of Bronfenbrenner (1979) and his ecological framework of child development. Brofenbrenner proposed an ecosystem of interconnections that facilitate the development of the child and highlighted the different, and equally important, roles players in the system have. The important thing about Bronfenbrenner's work is that it clearly showed that there is no one independent entity that ensures positive development of the child. It is cooperative systems and the interactions between them that result in healthy development. Perhaps most important in his model was the significance of mesosystems – the interactions between the different players in child development.

Undoubtedly, if we are to view the draft Online Safety Bill as the leading edge of online safeguarding law in the UK, this is something we have lost sight of in this area. By adapting this ecosystem for online safety, we can see both the breadth of stakeholder responsibilities for safeguarding, and how the stakeholders interact.

The value of the model is that is shows the many different stakeholders in online safeguarding and shows the importance of interactions (mesosystems) between them, as well as the distance a given stakeholder is from the child we wish to safeguard. There are many microsystems around the child, with whom the child directly interacts, before we even approach the place that technology provides in this safeguarding model. However, the focus of the vast majority of liability in legislation lies in an aspect of the exosystem – industry. This focus neglects a great many stakeholders that have a role to play in safeguarding, and fails to knowledge the contribution they could, and should, make.

Within this model we defined the UN Convention on the Rights of the Child (1989) as the fundamental macrosystem in which the entire stakeholder space is enveloped. This should be any policy maker's go-to for the development of new resources, technologies, policy or legislation. Yet this seems to be the most neglected, and often ignored, aspect of online child safeguarding. Arguably, it is sometimes viewed as a barrier to solutions, rather than the foundation of any legislative or policy development.

Where are we going?

In this chapter we have started to explore the influence of the joint Court of Protection judgments in *Re A* [2019] EWCOP 2 and *Re B* [2019] EWCOP 3, and the subsequent ruling in the appeal against the *Re B* judgment (EWCA Civ 913, 2019) on the world of adult safeguarding, and argued that while

Figure 2.1: Stakeholder model for child online safety

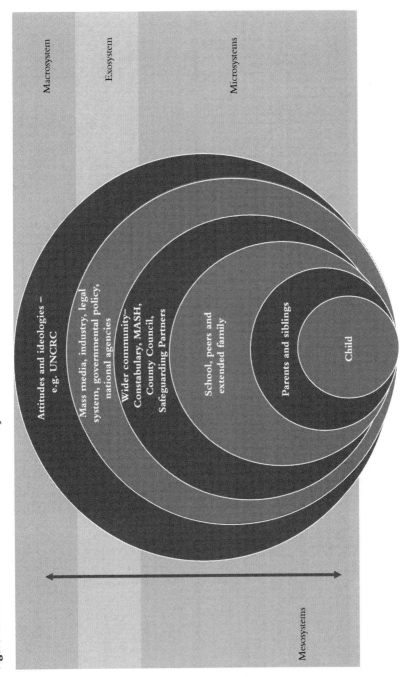

Source: Authors, based on Bronfenbrenner (1979)

it is admirable that Cobb J decided to explore the child online safeguarding world in order to develop his judgments, there is a risk that building upon this foundation could end up repeating the same mistakes of this area. We will return to the adult safeguarding world in the next chapter, where we will pick up on the Cobb J judgments, the tests he defines within them, and the subsequent legacy of the MCA.

3

Online participation vs protection and the Mental Capacity Act 2005

Introduction

This chapter covers the legal framework and legislative development which underpin the MCA, the Care Act 2014 (UK Government, 2014) and statutory guidance which sets out responsibilities for professionals working together. More specifically, it explores the legacy of the Cobb J 'rules', and how Court of Protection judgments have responded to issues of capacity to engage with the internet and social media since the tests have been introduced.

In drawing together these judgments and how the legal aspects of online safeguarding have been responded to in the Court of Protection, the chapter considers how the MCA contributes to safeguarding the best interests decision making for vulnerable adults in their online lives. It should be noted, however, that it is not intended to be a detailed exploration of the MCA; there are other texts that do an excellent job of this (for example Graham and Cowley, 2015). Equally, as set out in the introduction, this is not a text book – rather it encourages both academics and practitioners to think critically about the applicability of online 'safety' around adult safeguarding, particularly when supporting individuals with learning difficulties, under the umbrella of the MCA, and wider legislation, as well as Court of Protection rulings that have developed thinking from *Re A (Capacity: Social Media and Internet Use: Best Interests)* [2019] EWCOP 2 and *Re B (Capacity: Social Media: Care and Contact)* [2019].

The challenges of adult online safeguarding: the Mental Capacity Act 2005

One of the challenges we have observed, having worked for many years with professionals in the online safeguarding arena, is the practicalities of how to apply law and sometimes quite abstract guidance in real-world situations. With training we delivered to social care teams (discussed in more detail in Chapter 5), a recurring comment was, "Yes, we can see how everything has to happen on a case-by-case basis, and we are expected to be mindful of the best interests of the individual, but at the end of the day, what can we *practically* do to address this, given there is no guidance in the code of practice?" On top of the need for practical guidance, there were concerns that there are some aspects of working with individuals who lack capacity that can place those working with them at professional risk (see Chapter 7), and a culture of risk avoidance in organisations has arisen from the fear of criticism (Tindall, 2015), for example when talking to someone who wishes to access pornography when, perhaps, their parents or other care givers do not want them to. We explore this in more detail in Chapter 5, but it is worthwhile to highlight here because this particular issue forms the basis of our analysis around the Cobb J rulings in more detail, and why they were needed. Specifically:

- Is there anything in the MCA and Code of Practice to guide practitioners in making decisions around capacity to engage with online services?
- Do [2019] EWCOP 2 and [2019] EWCOP 3 address these concerns by professionals and provide them with evidence-informed support in making these decisions?

Given the historic age of the MCA (2005) and the Code of Practice, it is perhaps unsurprising that there is not specific mention of internet and social media use. Facebook was very much in its infancy and while 'the internet' was well established as a means for searching for information and messaging on platforms such as email, the general accessibility of technology that has allowed individuals to interact with each other, and to produce content, rather than consuming it, was not yet entering mass appeal. While the concept of 'Web 2.0' (O'Reilly, 2009) was first touted in 1999, it was not considered 'mainstream' even among the technology community until the first 'O'Reilly Media Web 2.0 Conference' at the end of 2004. Web 2.0, put simply, was the concept of the use of internet protocols to allow people to interact and contribute. 'Web 1.0' was very much a content consumption model, where search engines provided portals to the massive amount of information published online. However, the proportion of publishers to consumers was very heavily skewed towards consumers – without technical expertise and web hosting, being able to publish information was a challenge to the mainstream. Web 2.0 was, arguably, the advent of emerging technologies such as blogging, social media and 'sharing' sites (for example Youtube and Flickr) that allowed those without their own dedicated websites the means to contribute information, content and opinion online. Messaging platforms, which were the forerunners of platforms such as Facebook messenger and Snapchat, while being available in 2005, were predominantly the preserve of companies, used for informal communication among colleagues, rather than social messaging. Our first empirical work around the social use of messaging platforms and the social construction of *risk* (Beck, 1992; Giddens, 1990; 1991 online was in 2006 (see Lacohee et al, 2006; Bond, 2010; 2011;

2013; 2014) where we discussed the adoption of messaging platforms such as MSN and text messaging by children and young people and how their use was potentially exposing young people to harm, without the education or support to mitigate these risks.

Rulings considering online safeguarding

Therefore, it is hardly a surprise to see that specific consideration of online harms was not part of the MCA or the Code of Practice, and equally why it is important to consider not just the legislation, but also subsequent Court of Protection judgments that considered whether online activities were presenting risks that individuals perhaps did not have capacity to engage with unsupported. While [2019] EWCOP 2 and [2019] EWCOP 3 are considered to be 'seminal' in that this was the first time issues of capacity to engage with 'internet and social media' were considered in detail against the MCA and Court of Protection judgments, that is not to say concerns around capacity to engage have not been raised before. One judgment from the High Court and two from the Family Court are of particular interest here due, in the main, to the unsubstantiated concerns around internet access and why withdrawal of access would be a positive move for the individual of concern.

[2016] **EWHC 3473 (Fam)** – a case that considered deprivation of liberty of a young man, C, who lived in a residential unit under a number of restrictions, including no internet access and a locked mobile phone that only allowed calling to four numbers. While concern was raised in the analysis of the case that he sometimes 'accessed the internet and Facebook' without the consent of staff, and pushed boundaries, at no point was it explained what the specific risks associated with unrestricted access to the internet might bring; it was simply accepted that C's internet and mobile access should be controlled.

[2018] **EWFC 47** – another case around deprivation of liberty of a minor, RD, in care, which did not specifically focus upon any online issues but made the observation that '[i]nternet is available in the unit, but it is regulated by a safety feature which blocks social media and inappropriate sites; RD has access to an iPad on site; iPad use is not supervised; search histories are checked randomly'. Again, at no point is there any discussion around specific risks to RD that might arise from uncontrolled access to the internet, just that she does not have it. We should also note, in the quote, the view that because 'a safety feature' restricts access, no further consideration needs to be given, which both refers to our discussion in Chapter 2 around the efficacy of filters and is something we will explore in more detail in Chapter 4.

[2020] **EWHC 139 (Fam)** – a further deprivation of liberty order regarding a 16-year-old male, AK, who had, as noted in the judgment, a troubled childhood leading 'AK to a history of self-harm, suicidal ideation and low mood. He was in residential care and, in the words of the ruling, had AK has *unlimited* (emphasis in the original) access to and use of his mobile telephone, the internet and his Xbox'. The local authority was, among other requests for deprivation, asking for a change so AK could have no unsupervised access to the internet or a mobile phone. However, there is no explaination as to why this would be a beneficial restriction for AK and, indeed, the Children's Guardian raised concern, stating that

> despite arrangements that allow AK the freedom of unsupervised use of the Internet and telephone, unsupervised free time at home, unlocked doors and no room or person searches, AK has not self-harmed or demonstrated suicidal ideation, has not absconded and has engaged with the greater independence afforded to him in line with the social worker's expressed view of his needs. Within this context, the Children's Guardian submits that it is very difficult to see how an order that will have the effect of frustrating a similar placement for AK at [Z] can be said to be in his best interests or necessary and proportionate.

We explore in Chapter 6 in far more detail the assumed causations that can be brought to mental health issues, particularly self-harm, from internet access and we debunk some of these views. In this case the request for deprivation of liberty was rejected but it was interesting to note that the local authority wished to restrict internet access while making no case to explain why they wished to do this or why AK was more at risk if he retained unrestricted access. This was remarked upon by the presiding judge, MacDonald J, who said:

> In closing, I am bound also to observe that on the face of the papers there appears to be a stark contradiction in this case between the position of the local authority over the many, many months over which AK was repeatedly absconding, self-harming, committing crime and suffering with his mental health, during which time the local authority made no attempt to seek the relief for which it now contends, and the position now adopted by the local authority at the point that AK is showing improvement and progress, which is to press strenuously for relief that no longer adequately reflects AK's current position. It would be prudent for the local authority to reflect on this paradox.

While these three cases are all related to young people under the age of 18, they are all useful in considering how withdrawal of access can be called for without any evidence of the need. It seems from these rulings that it was the view of those wishing to withdraw access that it would simply be easier if the individual did not have access, just in case harm arose as a result.

Removal of online access, particularly from those in care or with disability, is not to be taken lightly. We recall a piece of work carried out by a young man with Autistic Spectrum Disorder (ASD) at an alternative provision unit with whom we were doing some work, who wrote a wonderful poster saying how, in the 'real world' he was a coward, scared of every little noise and over-stimulated by what went on in the world around him. However, he said, in his online worlds (predominantly using Minecraft to interact with gamers and cooperatively play) he could be a 'hero' and had 'friends all over the world'. While clearly there was some risk that some of those friends might not be who he thought they were, he was aware of those risks, understood them and did not interact with them outside of the gaming environment. Nevertheless, the fact that he gained a huge amount of benefit from his online world, which helped him with his disorder, was undeniable.

Drawing upon the MCA

While we have stated that there is nothing specific in the MCA, or the Code of Practice, that relates to the use of online technologies, that is not to say we cannot draw guidance from it. If we consider the MCA Code of Practice, it is clear that '[a] person's capacity must be assessed specifically in terms of their capacity to make a particular decision'. Court of Protection cases that consider behaviours related to the deprivation of liberty or capacity to engage with 'internet and social media' will generally have formed a question around 'Does P have capacity for internet and social media use?' (as is explored in far more detail in Chapter 4) or, if we reflect on questions asked of us by professionals the more problematic 'P has demonstrated they do not have capability to appreciate rule X of the Cobb judgments, therefore they have demonstrated they do not have capacity to engage with the internet and social media'. Clearly this is in conflict with a central premise of the MCA in that the best interests of the individual must be considered on a case-by-case basis. It further reinforces our concerns that, with a dearth of official guidance, or an updated MCA Code of Practice mindful of online risk, Cobb J's rulings will be used as 'law' rather than the stated intended aim as guidance in helping professional begin to make a judgement around capacity.

While we will return to the original and, in our view, problematic concept of 'internet and social media' later in this chapter, given its prevalence in both the Cobb judgments and also others from the Court of Protection, we will stay with the term for now (which is used interchangeably in other Court of Protection rulings as *social media and the internet)*.

If we consider internet and social media use specific to the MCA, we should be considering capacity to engage only when there is an identified risk or harm associated with this. This is not a case of 'if P engaged with social media there is a risk that they might meet someone they don't know and could potentially be exploited, therefore we need to test for capacity', there *should* be a need for evidence that there is risk of harm. Sections 5 and 6, for example, of the MCA state:

5. Acts in connection with care or treatment

(1) If a person ('D') does an act in connection with the care or treatment of another person ('P'), the act is one to which this section applies if—
   (a) before doing the act, D takes reasonable steps to establish whether P lacks capacity in relation to the matter in question, and
   (b) when doing the act, D reasonably believes—
      (i) that P lacks capacity in relation to the matter, and
      (ii) that it will be in P's best interests for the act to be done.
(2) D does not incur any liability in relation to the act that he would not have incurred if P—
   (a) had had capacity to consent in relation to the matter, and
   (b) had consented to D's doing the act.

6. Section 5 acts: limitations

(1) If D does an act that is intended to restrain P, it is not an act to which section 5 applies unless two further conditions are satisfied.
(2) The first condition is that D reasonably believes that it is necessary to do the act in order to prevent harm to P.
(3) The second is that the act is a proportionate response to—
   (a) the likelihood of P's suffering harm, and
   (b) the seriousness of that harm.
(4) For the purposes of this section D restrains P if he—
   (a) uses, or threatens to use, force to secure the doing of an act which P resists, or
   (b) restricts P's liberty of movement, whether or not P resists.

We could interpret this legislation literally and consider restriction to relate to physical restriction, and that restraint is necessary if P is at risk of physical harm. However, Cobb J's judgment, which we will return to in more detail later, makes specific mention of deprivation of internet access: 'I am conscious that a determination that a person lacks capacity to access and use the internet imposes a significant restriction upon his or her freedom.' We should also note the statement is section 5: 'D takes reasonable steps to establish whether P lacks capacity in relation to the matter in question.' Certainly, with our own work with professionals around adult online safeguarding, we doubt that 'reasonable steps' were always taken. We fear, in some cases, withdrawal of internet access, or excessive imposition of monitoring, was not done following reasonable steps or consideration of best interest, but because it was an 'easy' solution to potentially complex risk mitigation. If someone is *potentially* at risk of harm as a result of internet access, an easy solution is to withdraw internet access. However, as Cobb J points out in his judgments, this is something that places significant restrictions on an individual and should not be considered lightly.

Re A (Capacity: Social Media and Internet Use: Best Interests) [2019] EWCOP 2 and Re B (Capacity: Social Media: Care and Contact) [2019] EWCOP 3

In Chapter 2 we started to consider the impact of the *Re A* and *Re B* judgments of Cobb J and their impact on how we think about capacity to engage with 'internet and social media'. Given Cobb J made note of the use of child online safeguarding policy and practice in developing his thinking around these judgments, reviewing the context of online safeguarding helps us understand both where this thinking comes from and also the potential flaws in approaches. We now return to the judgments in more detail and consider the efficacy of the thinking and the early *legacy* of them, having, through our work in the social care sector, seen them often referred to in practice. We should stress, however, that this is an exploration of the judgments and how Cobb J came to define the six 'rules' that now pervade the adult online safeguarding world, particularly where issues of capacity are being discussed. It is useful to reflect on the approach taken by Cobb J in these rulings, and how the development of guidance around capacity to engage with the internet and social media is drawn from the child online safeguarding world because, just as we have observed, Cobb J felt there was nothing in adult safeguarding, either from practice or literature, that would underpin the development of the guidance. For reasons of space and fluidity of discussion, we do not reproduce the whole ruling here; it is in the public domain should readers wish to explore it in detail.

In reviewing the judgments it is pertinent to consider the salient facts in each case to understand how the judgments emerged. In the case of *A*, A was a 21-year-old male who identified as gay. He had mental capacity issues related to social and executive functioning and he would not have been able to manage his personal and domestic care needs without support. However, he had lived in independent supported accommodation for almost two years and had extensive social care to support him. His care team had concerns about his online use since early 2016, when he was still living at home.

His parents had discovered he was using social media to share intimate indecent photographs and videos and it was apparent that he had started to view extreme (illegal) pornography as a result of clicking through to such content from other (legal) sites. It was considered that he did not have the capacity or education to be able to use online services 'safely' and he had developed considerable interest in images of child abuse and other illegal pornography. His poor levels of literacy made it impossible for him to take heed of, or understand, the warnings regarding the content he was attempting to view. Again, the term 'safely' is an interesting one in this case – on the one hand sharing intimate images and videos does raise concerns for safety, given these behaviours can result in risk of exploitation and abuse. However, accessing illegal content is not a safety issue, it is one of legal risk and the potential for discovery and arrest by law enforcement. Keeping someone from accessing illegal content online is not a safety issue, it is one of liberty and criminal justice.

Previously A had disclosed he had been raped by an identified male and in the course of the investigation it became apparent he had built up an extensive collection of illegal pornography and indecent images of children, and had also contacted a large number of men, many of whom were identified by the police as sexual predators and offenders. It was the view of the investigating officer that if A's behaviour continued as it was, there was a risk that he could become a perpetrator of offences concerning possession of illegal content 'due to his lack of understanding around the subject'.

In the case of B, B was a 31-year-old adult female who struggled with personal care and hygiene and was prone to aggression when challenged. She lived at home but was assessed to require additional support to maintain her safety when communicating with others. She also became aggressive when receiving information she did not like. She was a frequent online technology user, via social media platforms Facebook and Snapchat, and personal messaging with WhatsApp. Over the previous three years her online behaviour had caused concern for her care worker as she was known to have used digital technology to send recipients intimate images of herself and excessively share personal information while attempting to meet strangers she had interacted with online. It was known she was keen to have a relationship and she would routinely progress from online introductions to intimate interactions with males. In one particularly concerning instance she had established a relationship with a known sex offender whom she claimed she intended to marry.

The cases shared a number of similarities, which is why Cobb J came to jointly rule on them. However, there were also differences: in the case of B there was no suggestion of her accessing illegal content or legal risk, it was very much concern around the potential for harm; for A, there was concern in terms of both risk of harm and risk of arrest.

The areas of interest, and some concern, for this analysis lie in the judicial interpretation of whether issues of online engagement differ from what could be considered to be general care, and how this might be tackled. We should state that the fact that this has been considered at the Court of Protection is to be applauded; we rarely see such consideration at this level in child online safeguarding, which seems to go through multiple iterations of different people coming up with the same prohibitive ideas. To see this level of consideration by the courts, especially with a focus on the best interests of individuals, is to be admired. However, as we have discussed in Chapter 2, consideration should be given to the foundations of Cobb J's thinking in understanding how the nature of online risk differs from risk of physical harm. It was Cobb J's view in *Re A* that engagement with online platforms does present novel challenges that have to be considered separate from more general care planning:

> 25. The first question on which I am asked to rule is whether, in undertaking a capacity assessment, internet and social media use should form a sub-set of a person's ability to make a decision about either 'contact' or 'care'. Having heard argument in this I have reached the clear view that the issue of whether someone has capacity to engage in social media for the purposes of online 'contact' is distinct (and should be treated as such) from general consideration of other forms of direct or indirect contact. I am satisfied that wider internet use is different from general issues surrounding care. There is a risk that if social media use and/or internet use were to be swept up in the context of care or contact, it would lead to the inappropriate removal or reduction of personal autonomy in an area which I recognise is extremely important to those with disabilities.

We would agree with the consideration of internet use and/or social media use having a different dimension to 'offline' contact, and also the importance of online access for those with disabilities. If one has physical or mental challenges that make engagement in offline situations challenging, the online world can offer opportunity for interaction. We are reminded of Mats Steen, whose Duchenne Muscular Dystrophy meant he was rarely able to leave his family home but who was engaged with a rich community of interaction through the online game World of Warcraft (Schaubert, 2019). It is very important to consider online interaction as something different, the lack of need to be physically in a space to take part in an interaction is an important one. Furthermore, issues of limitless geography, size of audience and 'always on' activity make it very different from offline experiences.

Cobb J's final judgment on the cases has resulted in sensible and pragmatic guidance for both cases. In the case of A, Cobb J ruled that the 'internet access and safety plan' put in place by the local authority (which provided limited, monitored and supervised internet access) was appropriate, while acknowledging A might seek to circumvent the measures put in place for monitoring (we will explore more around the efficacy of monitoring in Chapter 4). For B the judgment was clear that she was not sufficiently capacitous to use social media to meet people or develop relationships with them and that until should could demonstrate such capacity an interim declaration was necessary. Furthermore, he stated that should B remain unable to make decisions regarding social media use, it was perfectly acceptable to apply technical interventions (such as filtering and monitoring) to manage her social media use.

The implications of the rulings

We would not disagree with either of these judgments, which were considered and proportionate and moreover make clear reference to rights frameworks and legislation that is appropriate in considering the best interests of the individual:

- Impact on the individual's human rights, specifically Article 8 (right to respect for private and family life) and Article 10 (right to freedom of expression and information) ECHR (European Court of Human Rights, 1950).
- Article 21 (Freedom of expression and opinion) and Article 22 (Right to privacy) of the UNCRPD (United Nations, 2006).
- Section 1(6) of the MCA 2005 ('regard must be had to whether the purpose for which it is needed can be as effectively achieved in a way that is less restrictive of the person's rights and freedom of action').

As we have already explored with the stakeholder model in Chapter 2, the underpinning rights framework when considering child online safeguarding is the UN Convention of the Rights of the Child (UNCRC). There is no one comparable framework for vulnerable adults – the UNCRPD has some relevance and is acknowledged in the rulings but has nowhere near the level of ratification of the UNCRC. Similarly, again as acknowledged by Cobb J, the ECHR is another rights framework that can be drawn into discussions around capacity to engage with the internet and social media. While our focus in this text is how online safeguarding relates to the MCA and Court of Protection judgments relating to the capacity to use the internet and social media, it is worthwhile for practitioners to reflect upon the potential rights challenges that result from the withdrawal of access to online services, something of which they should be mindful when considering the best interests of the individual. We have defined the potential rights that are impacted in Table 3.1, drawn from both the ECHR and UNCRPD.

Table 3.1: Potential of rights impacted drawn from ECHR and UNCRPD

UNCRPD Article 12 – Equal recognition before the law	As we discuss in exploring Cobb J's guidance, there is a risk that, in applying this guidance as 'rules', a person with disability might be treated differently, legally speaking, from those without.
UNCRPD Article 14 – Liberty and security of the person ECHR Article 5 – The Right to Liberty and Security	Being online is now a fundamental part of having a full life, and removal of access to online services potential has impact upon liberty that need to be carefully considered with any capacity assessment.
UNCRPD Article 21 – Freedom of expression and opinion, and access to information ECHR Article 10 – Freedom of Expression	Clearly, if someone cannot go online, their opportunities for expression and access to information are severely restricted.
UNCRPD Article 22 – Respect for privacy ECHR Article 8 – The Right to Private and Family Life	As we will discuss in later chapters, safeguarding 'solutions' that excessively monitor a person's internet access, or spot-check their device, raise serious concerns around a right to privacy.
UNCRPD Article 24 – Education ECHR Protocol 1, Article 2 – The Right to Education	One thing that is stressed in the Cobb J rulings is that a person needs to be given the opportunity to understand the online risks they are facing before any decision about whether the person has capacity to engage with the internet and social media is made. Failure to do this potentially impacts on this right.
UNCRPD Article 29 – Participation in political and public life UNCRPD Article 30 – Participation in cultural life, recreation, leisure and sport	Without access to the internet, living a life full of active participation is challenging. This might be particularly true for a person with a disability whose mobility or capability to travel freely are restricted.
ECHR Article 14 – Prohibition of discrimination	As we will explore in some of the cases and in our discussions regarding professional judgements, it is important that an individual's disability is not used as a reason for a disproportionate response compared to an individual without disability, for example in a sensitive area such as access to pornography.

Source: Authors

However, as already expressed, we are concerned that the more general test laid out in the judgments reflects the passivity of the victims in the 3Cs while being an effective starting point when considering whether an adult with capacity issues might be considered capable of making effective judgements about their online engagements. Furthermore, we can also see, given our experiences in the child safeguarding arena, that there is a tendency to lack pragmatism when making safeguarding judgements in practice and instead to take advice and apply it as hard-set rules to apply to any given scenario.

Within his ruling, Cobb J set out a six-part test that would help those who needed to make safeguarding judgements on an individual's capacity to engage with 'internet and social media'.

The six parts of the test were defined in the *Re A* judgment as follows:

It is my judgment, having considered the submissions and proposals of the parties in this case and in Re B, that the 'relevant information' which P needs to be able to understand, retain, and use and weigh, is as follows:

1. Information and images (including videos) which you share on the internet or through social media could be shared more widely, including with people you don't know, without you knowing or being able to stop it;
2. It is possible to limit the sharing of personal information or images (and videos) by using 'privacy and location settings' on some internet and social media sites;
3. If you place material or images (including videos) on social media sites which are rude or offensive, or share those images, other people might be upset or offended;
4. Some people you meet or communicate with ('talk to') online, who you don't otherwise know, may not be who they say they are ('they may disguise, or lie about, themselves'); someone who calls themselves a 'friend' on social media may not be friendly;
5. Some people you meet or communicate with ('talk to') on the internet or through social media, who you don't otherwise know, may pose a risk to you; they may lie to you, or exploit or take advantage of you sexually, financially, emotionally and/or physically; they may want to cause you harm;
6. If you look at or share extremely rude or offensive images, messages or videos online you may get into trouble with the police, because you may have committed a crime.

Subsequent to the joint ruling, there was an appeal launched in the case of B by the Official Solicitor (as B's litigation friend) and a cross-appeal by the local authority heard by the Court of Appeal ([2019] EWCA Civ 913). Again, much of the scope of the appeal lies outside of the remit of this book (with focus on the capability of the local authority to carry out its safeguarding duties as a result of the ruling and whether B's human rights have been adversely restricted by the judgments) but there are some interesting comments made related to Cobb J's test, which share our concerns.

44. Whether the list or guideline of relevant information is shorter or longer, it is to be treated and applied as no *more than guidance* to be adapted to the facts of the particular case.

62. So far as concerns the appropriateness of the list, as in the case of the list specified by Cobb J in relation to a decision to use social media, we see no principled problem with the list provided that it is treated and applied as *no more than guidance to be expanded or contracted or otherwise adapted to the facts of the particular case.* (Emphasis added.)

This is the crux of any guidance: it should only ever be considered measured advice. However, whether it will be applied as such or will be used as hardwired rules to exclude a person with mental capacity issues from exercising their fundamental rights to access digital services unless they can in some way have a detrimental effect on their well-being remains to be seen. Within our work in online safeguarding, we have often seen absolutist positions and value biases being used as justification for punitive action or withdrawal of access. The three examples we provided in Chapter 2 are all illustrations of this, and we have seen many more in the child online safeguarding world. Simple statements such as 'they shouldn't be on social media at this age' expose an attitude that the fault of harm lies with a victim of abuse because they are engaging with a service which is, in the eye of the professional, 'illegal' for them to access. While there are laws that relate to age limits on social media (usually the age limit is 13), these are not, as we are often told, anything to do with safeguarding. There is nothing in child development to suggest that a 12-year-old is incapable of making risk-free judgements on their use of an online service and a 13 year old is capable of doing so. Instead, these laws (specifically the Data Protection Act 2018 (UK Government, 2018) in the UK, an implementation of the EU's General Data Protection Regulation (European Union, 2016) and the Children's Online Privacy Protection Act (Federal Trade Commission, 1998) in the US relate to the capability of the individual to consent to data processing being carried out on their personal data.

However, regardless of the legislation, and with the façade of safeguarding legislation removed, we would counter that the safeguarding professional's first concern should not be the legal age of engagement, but the disclosure of concern or harm by the child. This is something will we return to in more detail in Chapter 5. Given our experiences over the years working in the safeguarding world, a concern we have is this test being seen as an absolute evaluation, rather than guidance used to help a judgement based upon these assessments that are unique to any given individual. Reviewing Cobb J's guidance, we are minded to think how many capacitous individuals would be capable, if assessed, of being able to recognise the risks in this list. By way of illustration, if we take point 6 of the six-part test, related to extreme pornography, the legal case book grows ever larger in relation to extreme pornography prosecutions of those individuals without mental capacity issues who are not aware of the illegality of the images, or even that they had retained images (BBC News, 2019a and Eleftheriou-Smith, 2014).

In the case of Ticehurst and Kelly (Eleftheriou-Smith, 2014), the clearly capacitous individuals claimed in their defence that they were not aware the media of which they were in possession was illegal and they were equally not aware they were retained on their device even after deletion from the messaging app. In the 2019 Glew case (BBC News 2019a) the presiding judge went so far as to say he felt the approach used was a sledgehammer to crack a 'very small' nut and questioned the public interest in prosecuting someone for this sort of possession. More recently, there has been media coverage of Robyn Novlett's case, where she was found in possession of a child abuse video on her phone, sent to her from her sister, who received it from her boyfriend. Ms Novlett, who was an acting police chief superintendent at the time of charge, was found guilty of being in possession, received a community service order, and was dismissed from her job. However, she was later reinstated (BBC News, 2021), having claimed that she was not aware the video was on her phone, as WhatsApp will store a media file even if it has not been opened or viewed by the recipient. This is a clear illustration, we suggest, that these tests are only useful if applied with pragmatism by knowledgeable and well-trained individuals. If, in all of the earlier examples, these capacitous individuals had been subject to Cobb J's test, they would clearly have failed at point 6. If applied as an absolute, it could be argued that their rights to internet access should be supervised or restricted because they had demonstrated that they lacked capacity.

As mentioned earlier, if we reflect upon our time working in the online child safeguarding space, we can see emerging parallels with growing concerns for vulnerable adults and internet access – technology is viewed as the solution and practitioners are looking for simple guidance that can be uniformly applied. We fear that the online adult safeguarding space risks becoming part of the *safeguarding dystopia* (Phippen, 2016) manifested among children and young people by professionals wishing to keep them *safe*.

There is much to be welcomed in Cobb J's judgments, and there was a hope that they would provide much-needed guidance for practitioners, with the caveat that it should be viewed as just that. However, at the time of the judgments there were concerns in the community (ourselves included) that there was a likelihood that the guidance would be interpreted as 'rules'. It was clear in Cobb J's ruling that the guidance was not a hard-and-fast set of rules to be applied in all tests and in the event of failure digital rights be withdrawn. This is just part of the need to develop a stakeholder approach that requires informed, well-trained professionals treating each individual as such, and having the knowledge and understanding to support their clients to use social media rather than applying blanket rules, looking for easy solutions and failing to consider the best interest of the vulnerable adult.

As we have discussed earlier, of course it would be easier for care teams to remove internet access completely – there would be far less risk to the individual then! However, such an approach rides roughshod over the rights of the individual and does not address the specific mental capacity issue, failing to align with the MCA Code of Practice or sections 5 and 6 of the legislation. There appear to be two somewhat polarised approaches at present: either the care team allows individuals with mental capacity issues access to online services, or it withdraws them. We would propose there is a third way, alluded to in Cobb J's interim order regarding B. In the same way that care teams might help an individual to learn about how to manage financial affairs or personal hygiene, should the teams be equipped to develop their clients' understanding of how to be able to use online services effectively, to understand the risks and where to go for help if things go wrong? Given the United Nations have stated that internet access is now a human right (United Nations, 2016), we would hope that those with mental capacity issues can be empowered to engage with online services and all the benefits they bring. This does, of course, raise training issues for those with responsibility for the care of those with mental capacity issues. However, we feel this is a middle ground that is more empowering and progressive, and more likely to result in those with mental capacities being able to use online services with reduced risk, rather than just allowing them to do what they like, or withdrawing their access.

Conclusion

In this chapter we have considered the challenges of online safeguarding for vulnerable adults and explored aspects of the MCA that give practitioners guidance on how it might be applied in these contexts. However, we acknowledge that a piece of legislation receiving royal assent in 2005 will certainly not be mindful of modern online issues, and we have seen both the High Court and Family Courts considering these issues. However, the [2019] EWCOP 2 and [2019] EWCOP 3 rulings create a watershed for those working under the auspices of the MCA and for the first time provide guidance to practitioners on how they might consider capacity to engage with the internet and social media. However, these rulings are built upon the protectionist discourses of online child safeguarding and, as such, are not without flaw. We fear that, when applied without the pragmatism Cobb

J calls for, we may be setting the bar for capacity higher than that which is afforded to the population as a whole. In the next chapter we consider the legacy of these rulings in detail, to draw out the emergent issues, both good and bad, that develop Court of Protection thinking on matters around capacity to engage with the internet and social media.

The legacy of *Re A* and *Re B*

Introduction

As we observed earlier in this book, the goal of this analysis is not to suggest that the Court of Protection is failing in its judgments, or basing judgments on ignorance. However, it does provide an opportunity to highlight how a single (joint) ruling, which itself admits to drawing from knowledge in a not specifically relevant discipline (given that child safeguarding is very different from both statutory and rights-based perspectives), then becomes *law* for further judgments, and is further applied in a manner which Cobb J specifically said it should not be. In this exploration we consider the rulings of a number of Court of Protection judgments that are influenced by Cobb J's rulings and explore how the complex issue of capacity to engage with the internet and social media can present challenges when applying the MCA, being mindful of best interests, how value biases can be brought to these rulings, and how thinking is now moving on from general capacity to engage to consider how problematic engagements might be managed while not withdrawing all rights to engage with online services.

This is a detailed chapter that looks at a number of rulings in turn, considering the online safeguarding issues explored within them, before discussion of the legacy of *Re A* and *Re B* and the impact on adult online safeguarding practice.

[2019] EWCOP 57

This ruling is not specific to access to the internet and social media, but there are elements of the ruling that consider this and also raise questions as to who decides the risk that leads to a decision about capacity (and if there is any risk identified at all). This ruling, presided over by Sir Mark Hedley, concerns PWK, a 24-year-old male who has spent a lot of time in the care system, and who has autism, mild learning disability and a visual impairment. At the time of the judgment he was living in shared accommodation, with care provided by a private organisation. Sir Mark noted that PWK had told him he was happy with this arrangement.

The nature of the judgment was to consider an application by the local authority to seek declarations of capacity which would have impact upon

PWK's liberty. This request arose because the care package offered to PWK had impact upon his liberty and there was a need to consider whether PWK had capacity to consent to deprivation:

4. The package of support, which includes two-to-one supervision, undoubtedly involves a deprivation of liberty. If PWK has the requisite capacity then, of course, he can consent to that deprivation. If, however, he does not have that capacity, then his deprivation of liberty needs to be authorised. His present accommodation is not a care home so the statutory scheme under Schedule A1 of the Mental Capacity Act 2005 does not apply. This deprivation of liberty requires the authorisation of the Court under Section 16 of that Act. Accordingly, questions as to his capacity arise. A finding that PWK lacks the relevant capacity is the only gateway which allows the Court to make best interest decisions and to grant authorisations. That is so even where, as here, there are no realistic alternatives to what is provided and the person concerned is in fact content with the arrangements.

5. The applicant Local Authority seeks declarations of incapacity in six areas: first, where to reside; secondly, care and support needs; thirdly, contact with others; fourthly, social media and the internet; fifthly, financial and property affairs; and lastly, use or possession of his car provided by the Motability scheme.

What is entirely missing from the analysis presented in the judgment, however, is any specific mention of why access to social media and the internet would present risk to PWK, something that could have been straightforward to explain while maintaining PWK's anonymity in this judgment. We acknowledge that specific detail about an individual regarding a judgment should be omitted from public record to avoid the potential for identification (for example in the event of media coverage of legal cases), but given the realiance on Court of Protection judgments to move forward practice around making judgements around capacity and deprivation of liberty, it is useful to see the general rationale for a statement as to why a declaration of lack of capacity is needed, rather than to simply state this is what is being asked. As we discuss later in this chapter, the broad nature of 'capacity to access the internet and social media' is, of itself, problematic, and slowly judgments are bringing more of a focus onto capacity to engage with specific online practices. A simple claim of 'they do not have capacity to engage with the internet and social media' is worthy of some clarification.

There is an implication that it might relate to 'harmful content'. In Sir Mark's consideration of capacity (making use of the [2019] EWCOP 2 ruling by Cobb J), he states:

27. I have considered, with care, the observations made by Cobb J in Re A (Capacity: Social Media and Internet Use: Best Interests) [2019] EWCOP 2. In my judgment, it is correct to make a separate determination in this case as well. I am satisfied, again applying a longitudinal perspective, that PWK lacks capacity in this area. Just as PWK is undoubtedly able to make choices as to what he wears or what he eats, so he will be able to make many choices in this area, but not all and *in particular he lacks the ability to make judgments about what is actually harmful as opposed to merely unpleasant and some judgments will simply have to made for him.* (Emphasis added.)

Sir Mark continues that while capacity to access the internet and social media is in his judgement lacking, he goes on to state '[a]gain, I think it both unwise and unnecessary to say more for all the indications are that these matters can be negotiated and resolved on the ground'.

As discussed earlier we find this judgment troubling because, first, there is no explanation of what the specific harms might be, or any evidence that PWK has been subject to online risk in the past as a result of a lack of capacity. It seems to be concerning that withdrawal of access to the internet and social media can be expressed without further explanation or evidence of harm.

If we consider [2019] EWCOP 2 or [2019] EWCOP 3, there is very clear evidence of both A and B having engaged in harmful and, in the case of A, criminal behaviour, using digital technology. All that we have with this judgment is a mention of the fact that PWK ' [in] particular ... lacks the ability to make judgments about what is actually harmful as opposed to merely unpleasant'.

We have discussed earlier whether the tests set out by Cobb J might lead to applications which present those with capacity issues with a higher bar than those who do not. We would assume that this comment might relate to both rules 5 and 6 of the Cobb J judgment, related to deception online and harmful content. However, Sir Mark makes comment about harmful content, rather than illegal or criminal (there is no suggestion in the ruling that PWK has ever accessed illegal content).

The concept of *legal but harmful* has been subject of much debate in the online safeguarding arena, and we have covered some of these issues in Chapter 2. While there has been attempt to define what this might be for children and young people (for example in the Department for Education's *Keeping Children Safe in Education* statutory guidance (DfE, 2018)), and the UK Safer Internet Centre's supplementary advice on 'appropriate' filtering and monitoring (UK Safer Internet Centre, 2021a; 2021b).

However, far less attention has been paid to what might be considered 'legal but harmful' for adults, until the introduction of the draft Online Safety

Bill 2021. This is actually considered for the first time in a legal Bill, and we include the section of the Bill (s 46) that considers content that might be harmful to adults in full:

46 Meaning of 'content that is harmful to adults' etc

(1) This section applies for the purposes of this Part.
(2) 'Content that is harmful to adults', in relation to a Category 1 service, means content that is—
   (a) regulated content in relation to that service, and
   (b) either—
      (i) of a description designated in regulations made by the Secretary of State as priority content that is harmful to adults (see section 47), or
      (ii) within subsection (3) or (5).
(3) Content is within this subsection if the provider of the service has reasonable grounds to believe that the nature of the content is such that there is a material risk of the content having, or indirectly having, a significant adverse physical or psychological impact on an adult of ordinary sensibilities ('A').
(4) For the purposes of subsection (3), in the case of content which may reasonably be assumed to particularly affect people with a certain characteristic (or combination of characteristics), or to particularly affect a certain group of people, the provider is to assume that A possesses that characteristic (or combination of characteristics), or is a member of that group (as the case may be).
(5) Content is within this subsection if the provider of the service has reasonable grounds to believe that there is a material risk of the fact of the content's dissemination having a significant adverse physical or psychological impact on an adult of ordinary sensibilities, taking into account (in particular)—
   (a) how many users may be assumed to encounter the content by means of the service, and
   (b) how easily, quickly and widely content may be disseminated by means of the service.
(6) Where the provider has knowledge, relevant to the content, about a particular adult at whom content is directed, or who is the subject of it, subsections (3) and (5) are to be read as if the reference to an adult of ordinary sensibilities were a reference to that particular adult, taking into account any of the following things that are known to or inferred by the provider—
   (a) that adult's characteristics;
   (b) that adult's membership of a certain group of people.

(7) The reference in subsection (3) to a risk of content 'indirectly' having a significant adverse physical or psychological impact on an adult is a reference to a risk of either of the following—

   (a) content causing an individual to do or say things to a targeted adult that would have a significant adverse physical or psychological impact on such an adult;

   (b) content causing an adult to act in a way that—

      (i) has a significant adverse physical or psychological impact on that adult, or

      (ii) increases the likelihood of such an impact on that adult.

(8) For the purposes of this section—

   (a) illegal content (see section 41) is not to be regarded as within subsection (3) or (5), and

   (b) content is not to be regarded as within subsection (3) or (5) if the risk of physical or psychological impact flows from—

      (i) the content's potential financial impact,

      (ii) the safety or quality of goods featured in the content, or

      (iii) the way in which a service featured in the content may be performed (for example, in the case of the performance of a service by a person not qualified to perform it).

(9) 'Priority content that is harmful to adults' means content of a description designated as such in regulations under subsection (2)(b).

(10) In relation to a Category 1 service, the terms 'content that is harmful to adults' and 'priority content that is harmful to adults' are to be taken to include material which, if it were present on the service, would be content within the definition in question (and this section is to be read with such modifications as may be necessary for that purpose).

(11) In this section 'targeted adult', in relation to content, means an adult—

   (a) who is the subject of the content, or

   (b) who is a member of a class or group of people with a certain characteristic (or combination of characteristics) targeted by the content.

We include this in full not to encourage readers to engage with the full 145-page draft Bill, but to illustrate the complexity of what might be defined as harmful for adults. It is extremely complex to try to encapsulate everything that *could* be harmful to an adult, and could encompass all manner of different forms of content that could cause 'a significant adverse physical or psychological impact on an adult of ordinary sensibilities'. Furthermore, and certainly not for this book, there needs to be far more detailed consideration of what an 'adult of ordinary sensibilities' is. Nevertheless, in this ruling, we are seeing PWK's access to the internet and social media potentially being withdrawn with a simple statement of concern around PWK's capacity to appreciate the different between unpleasant and harmful. We would anticipate that what is harmful to adults will be the subject of much legal debate in the coming years and it seems somewhat unfair to decide PWK lacks capacity on the basis that he might not be able to appreciate this clearly.

We note that Sir Mark states that the specifics of online engagement can be 'negotiated and resolved on the ground'. We assume that these negotiations will happen with the care team provided by the private provider, or local authority staff. As we have already discussed, and something we will explore in far more detail in Chapter 5, we do necessarily have confidence that professionals who are engaged in those negotiations would have had sufficient, or indeed any, training in online safeguarding and therefore may perhaps bring value bias rather than professional judgement to the resolutions.

Furthermore, and finally, there is nothing in this ruling that describes any potential education package that has been put in place for PWK to help him better distinguish between unpleasant and harmful content online. While we acknowledged the ambiguities of harmful content earlier, educational intervention might at least provide PWK with the means to be able to demonstrate more effective risk mitigation, which might subsequently allow him to demonstrate capacity.

[2019] EWCOP 64

This judgment concerned a 31-year-old woman, referred to in the document as Mary, who has learning disability that impacts on both social and functional skills, and cognitive impairments. She was assessed as suffering from Emotionally Unstable Personality Disorder and Dependent Personality Disorder. She lived in supported residential care.

The application brought by the local authority for the Court to determine was Mary's capacity in a range of aspects of her life, including accessing the internet and social media. Evidence was presented that Mary was at risk of harm, and injunctions had already been taken out against two individuals, one of whom had been in a sexual relationship with Mary. The case was considered by HHJ George.

The case is of interest because it refers to the Cobb J rules, stating that 'Mr Justice Cobb's formulation in this domain was approved' and listing the 'rules' without further comment. The case also makes a specific, detailed assessment of Mary's access to the internet and social media, arguing why she should does not have capacity. It differs greatly from [2019] EWCOP 57 in that it presents a strong rationale for the lack of capacity, based upon an assessment carried out by a social worker who had worked with Mary in the past:

16. I now turn to the evidence. I have a number of capacity assessments undertaken by Ms Clark, the social worker who has known Mary for quite some time. Those assessments were undertaken in 2019 and deal with Mary's capacity to make decisions about residence, care, use of social media, consenting to sexual relations and contact.

The assessment of Mary's capacity to make decisions about social media:

(a) Mary's history of being subjected to prolonged childhood abuse is noted to have had a considerable effect on her functioning and in particular in her being able to identify and measure risks.

(b) Mary trusts her online 'friends' because she has chatted to them for a long time and they look nice.

(c) Her understanding of how the internet works is extremely limited.

(d) Mary is unable to assess that there is any risk in allowing known sex offenders to access the internet using her device rather than their own. She does not understand that she may be committing a criminal offence in doing this.

Mary is unable to understand that there is any risk to her from her use of social media and the internet. In particular she does not understand that there is a risk to her in providing her associates (who are sex offenders) with the passwords to her Facebook accounts and that in doing so she may be committing a criminal offence.

(f) Mary lacks the ability to retain the information about the risks that on-line activity can create, despite being given this information in the safety of a psychology session.

(g) Accordingly, Mary lacks the capacity to decide to use social media.

Ultimately, HHJ George ruled that Mary did not have capacity to engage with the internet or social media, stating 'I am satisfied, on the balance of probabilities, that Dr Lawson's evidence is that Mary is not always able to understand the relevant information, particularly when making decisions about contact and social media'. However, when considering the evidence that Mary lacked capacity to engage with social media, we would question this assessment. While there is an argument being made that Mary can potentially place herself at risk due to being too trusting of online 'friends' and not recognising risk, there are specific concerns with the claims made:

(c) Her understanding of how the internet works is extremely limited.

We would argue this is certainly the case for the majority of internet users. While it is not clear exactly what is meant in this case, as it is not clearly detailed, we would draw an analogy with driving a car – very few individuals have a detailed understanding of an internal combustion engine yet they are still capable of driving a car.

(d) Mary is unable to assess that there is any risk in allowing known sex offenders to access the internet using her device rather than their own. She does not understand that she may be committing a criminal offence in doing this.

Providing access to a device is not a criminal offence; it would, however, invalidate the terms and conditions of access to online services. There is a risk that in providing offenders with access to her device, those offenders might conduct illegal activity on the device (for example accessing indecent images of a minor) that might place Mary at risk if such activity were detected. But the statement that allowing someone else to access your device is criminal is wholly inaccurate.

(e) Mary is unable to understand that there is any risk to her from her use of social media and the internet. In particular she does not understand that there is a risk to her in providing her associates (who are sex offenders) with the passwords to her Facebook accounts and that in doing so she may be committing a criminal offence.

Again, sharing one's social media passwords is not a criminal offence. If that were the case many couples across the country would be subject to criminal investigation! Again, there is a risk someone might use access to a social media account to engage in criminal activity. However, this is more difficult to do on a social media platform with its many filtering and control features.

(f) Mary lacks the ability to retain the information about the risks that on-line activity can create, despite being given this information in the safety of a psychology session.

This implies that there might have been some effort to explain online risk to Mary and that she had failed to retain this information. However, it does not say how this information was articulated or whether it was reinforced. It feels a little like 'we've told her once, and she doesn't get it'. We would question whether Mary had been given reasonable opportunity to learn.

[2019] EWCOP 66

While this judgment does not specifically refer to the Cobb J rulings, there is relevance in terms of the interest in engaging with 'internet and social media', demonstrating that this, as a term, was becoming embedded into practice around capacity assessments. The ruling specifically dealt with a police request to access psychological reports regarding an individual, AB, who is subject to proceedings in the Court of Protection. AB, who is described in the ruling as 'immensely vulnerable', was also subject to a police investigation where, between 2017 and 2018, they had committed offences related to accessing category C images of children. No further details of the offence were given but the police were asking for access to the expert reports, from which, if they concluded that, at the time of the offences, AB did not have capacity to access the 'internet and social media', then criminal proceedings against AB would likely be discontinued. However, it was also stated that if the request for access was refused, the police would call for a separate expert to carry out an assessment of AB's capacity.

The ruling is also of interest because it shows that capacity to access the internet and social media might be evolving into a simplistic test of whether an individual might be charged with criminal activity for a *specific* online act. Moreover, there is an assumption that a simple test is all that is needed to determine capacity, which can then be applied to any situation, at any given time.

Keehan J, in his ruling, makes specific mention of the timeliness of the request:

10. The third report does touch upon the issue of AB's capacity to access the internet and social media but that assessment was reached after AB had undergone a programme of education to assist him to have capacity to make that particular decision. The assessment of the psychologist was that in May 2019, AB did have capacity to access the internet and social media. This third report does not deal with the question of whether AB had capacity on this issue in 2017 and 2018, the period covered by the index offences for which AB is charged. Accordingly, in my judgment, that third report contains nothing of relevance to the police investigation other than for the police to know that:

a. prior to coming to a conclusion, the expert had arranged for AB to undergo educative work; and
b. that her assessment that, in May 2019, AB had the capacity to access the internet and social media, was limited to that time and in the context of the educative work undertaken with him.

And as such, he could not see how the disclosure of the report would be of benefit to either the police or to AB, and was also mindful of the rights of AB as a subject of the Court of Protection:

12. It is, in my judgment, supremely important that those who are the subject of the Court of Protection are as frank as they possibly can be

to those who are seeking to assess them and, accordingly, I would only consider disclosing the expert's report to the police if the weight to be given to the public interest was so great as to outweigh the consideration of frankness by AB in the Court of Protection proceedings. As it is, I have come to the conclusion that the expert's reports are not relevant to the issue that the police have to determine for the purposes of the prosecution of AB, namely between 2017 and 2018, did AB have capacity to access the internet and social media? As I have already said, the expert does not address that issue in any of her reports.

While it would seem from the reading of the ruling that the police intention was an honourable one – suggesting that if lack of capacity could be demonstrated, then criminal proceedings would be discontinued – it does suggest the interpretation was one where if someone was considered not to have capacity, they could never have had capacity. With the alleged crimes taking place before the assessment, Keehan J's conclusion that the report could be no help to the police should surely have been something that could have been determined without the need for a court ruling. If crimes took place before an assessment had taken place, we cannot simply assume that if someone was not capacitous in 2019, they would not have been in 2017 either.

However, one encouraging observation to draw from the ruling is the efficacy of education intervention in supporting those who might have capacity issues. While the nature of the education programme was not detailed in the ruling, we can, if considering the rights of AB independently of the criminal proceedings, see a positive outcome in that after AB had undertaken an education programme, it was considered that AB did have capacity to access the internet and social media:

> 3. For the purpose of preparing the capacity assessment on accessing the internet and social media, AB underwent an education programme in relation to decision-making relating to accessing the internet and social media. It was after he had undergone that programme that the psychologist prepared her third and final report in which she concluded that at that time, that is May 2019, *AB had capacity to access the internet and social media.* (Emphasis in the original.)

[2020] EWCOP 24

In this case, heard by Cobb J, a local authority were seeking declarations and orders so that they could effectively safeguard an individual while being mindful of his best interests. The individual in this case was AW, a 35-year-old man living in residential care, who had learning disabilities and autism. The case is of interest first because, being heard by Cobb J, it allows us to explore how his own thinking have developed since [2019] EWCOP 2 and [2019] EWCOP 3. While there is little to disagree with in the judgment, the case is interesting to examine from the perspective of *safety protocols* as a means of providing access in a controlled manner. It is also a case that predominately considers issues of capacity to engage with social media and the internet and should be considered important for this reason.

Concerns for AW arose from his meeting of men he had met online and harm that occurred as a result. AW had a history of harm – he was sexually assaulted by a man he had met online in 2009 and, in 2012, involved in accusations of inappropriate behaviour with a minor. Social workers provided evidence that AW often placed himself at risk as a result of meeting men through dating sites online, as well as the 'fallout' from when relationships or encounters formed in this way failed. It was disclosed that in 2018 AW had assaulted his mother when she did no allow him to use her laptop to go online, and also assaulted staff at his residential home. He had also been assaulted himself through these encounters and run up debt as a result of being online frequently.

As Cobb J commented in the ruling, it was clear that there was a lot of evidence in his history to highlight AW's lack of understanding of risk and harm:

> 13. Even the short extracts of AW's relevant history above give an indication of AW's poor understanding of social boundaries and the risks involved in him meeting strangers, particularly after a very short introduction on the web, without having made any rudimentary assessment of those risks. AW's vulnerability is further underlined by him sending inappropriate pictures of himself to strangers. Unsurprisingly perhaps he is assessed by his carers as being 'vulnerable to exploitation'.

However, further comments as a result of talking to AW show perhaps an unfounded concern: '14. He is said generally to be very happy at Windmill Lodge, though because he has spent many hours at night on the Internet and on his phone, he tends to sleep all day, missing activities; this has caused him to become somewhat socially isolated.' AW would certainly not be the only adult who spends too much time online in the evening with this impact upon their daytime activities. However, further observations from a key social worker demonstrate a good understanding of AW's needs and how he lacks capacity in some aspects of his online life:

> 15. I have three detailed statements from the key social worker. She has been commended by LJ [AW's mother] for her sensitive work with AW. She has commented as follows:
> 'AW is driven by a desire to have a relationship; he will often view people he has only just made contact with briefly as being a "friend"

or "boyfriend". This desire has often led him to engage in risky behaviour. ... Without consideration of his own welfare or other possible consequences of his actions.

Another risk associated with AW's use of the Internet is that he will become upset and aggressive if he feels he has been rejected by someone he has just met who he views as a boyfriend or potential boyfriend. ... AW is not able to understand social cues and lacks insight into the emotions and intentions of others.

It is clear that due to his "social blindness" AW is unable to understand other people's motives or social cues. He has no understanding of the possible implications of his behaviour in the community as well as understanding the risks on the use of the Internet to seek out sexual relationships.'

The judgment also makes note of the fact that use of the internet and social media is already limited in the care home, where AW is given one-to-one supervision when accessing the internet (permitted once per day) and not allowed further online devices. The local authority had conducted risk assessments specific to AW's needs, demonstrating again that they were mindful of both the risks associated with AW going online, but also his human rights and best interests.

Unsurprisingly, Cobb J makes reference to [2019] EWCOP 3 in considering AW's capacity:

26

(iii) On use of social media and the internet (applying Re A (capacity: social media and internet) [2019] EWCOP 3):

'although AW understood some of the relevant information in the area, I do not believe he understood how vulnerable his behaviour makes him on the internet. He has limited strategies to keep himself safe and has no insight into the impact that being on the internet for hours will have on his mental well-being. ... AW's overwhelming need to use the internet has an adverse impact on his ability to weigh-up the positives and negatives of using the internet';

Point (iv) within the same paragraph also makes reference to AW's capacity to understand the risks associated with sharing personal information that has relevance to his use of online technology:

(iv) On making decisions about sharing personal information:

'It is my opinion that AW failed to understand the risks associated with sharing personal information and could not weigh-up the positives and negatives of doing this';

Unsurprisingly, Cobb J came to the conclusion that AW did lack capacity to make decisions as to contact with others and access and use of the internet and social media. However, being mindful of AW's best interests, this was not an absolute removal of access to the internet and social media and, instead, Cobb J ordered that the approach the local authority had used to support AW accessing the internet to meet and date should remain in place:

> 52. I further find, and shall so order, that:
>
> (i) It is in AW's best interests to receive care and support in accordance with his assessed needs at [Windmill House];
> (ii) It is in AW's best interests to receive care and support in accordance with his care and support plan dated 10 March 2020 and the protocol to support his use of the internet;

In this comprehensive judgment, there was also consideration of the use of education to support AW so that the approach would not have to be quite as restrictive. However, comment was made that this approach did not work because of AW's condition:

> 34. In answer to the question at [33](i) above, Dr Rippon was specifically asked whether any 'practicable steps' could be taken now to assist AW to attain capacity in this area; she replied:
> 'I tried to provide him with education, but it didn't improve his understanding. ... It is a fundamental aspect of his autistic spectrum disorder and I don't think that it could be improved by education'.

This echoed an earlier passage from her report:

> 'I am aware that a considerable amount of work has been undertaken with AW by his current care team and this has had no impact on his capacity in the areas which I have been asked to consider. At interview, AW himself acknowledged that nothing which staff had done had stopped him wanting to use the internet and meet men. I cannot suggest any therapeutic intervention or educational package that would result in him gaining capacity.'

This is a thorough judgment which considers all of the potential support that could be offered to AW and, in the event that he was judged not to have capacity, was still mindful to provide some supportive access. Clearly Cobb J was still mindful of the comment made in [2019] EWCOP 2 regarding deprivation of access to the internet: 'I am conscious that a determination that a person lacks capacity to access and use the internet imposes a significant restriction upon his or her freedom.'

[2020] EWCOP 29

This case concerned a young adult male, RS, who was in his mid 20s. He had a diagnosis of autism and mild learning disability and had been exposed to a number of traumatic life events, listed as domestic abuse, alcohol abuse, bereavement and inappropriate sexual activity. At the time of the judgment RS lived in a supported placement funded by the local authority. The case was heard by MacDonald J, and concerned an application by the local authority to determine whether, among other activities, RS had capacity to access the internet and social media.

The case is of interest because it is, as acknowledged by MacDonald J, 'borderline' between someone placing themselves at risk and needing protection, and the freedom of sexual expression by an individual with learning difficulties. We can see from some of the evidence given in the case that concern might arise not just for concern for the individual, but also value biases by those with caring responsibilities around the acceptability of these practices. Specifically, the ruling set out RS's sexual fetish around infantilism:

> 7. RS has a sexual fetish, namely paraphilic infantilism, also referred to as ABDL (an acronym for adult baby/diaper lovers). This fetish involves adults role-playing a regression to an infant-like state, including the wearing of nappies. Such conduct is not, subject to the ordinary boundaries delineated by the criminal law, unlawful. The local authority contends however, and the Official Solicitor accepts that his fetish leads RS, in the exploration of his sexuality, to engage in risky behaviour, including *contacting males on the Internet and thereafter going to meet them*. (Emphasis added.)

The local authority provided a number of instances which they claimed demonstrated that RS placed himself at risk while engaging with this fetish:

(i) On 26 February 2018 RS went to stay with a male in Scotland and revealed, some weeks later, that the man was a registered sex offender who had forced RS to engage in sex.

(ii) Between April and May 2018 RS made contact with a number of men not previously known to him and expressed a wish to visit them. RS does not appeared to have visited any of those men but did purchase tickets with a view to doing so.

(iii) In July 2018 RS went to stay with a male and engaged in further contact with unknown men.

(iv) In August 2018 RS was the victim of alleged financial abuse, sending money to men that he had met online.

(v) In January 2019 RS brought a sixteen year old young man back to his flat.

(vi) On 14 February 2019 it was discovered that RS had been scammed resulting in him handing over a substantial amount of money to a couple via a fetish website, continuing to send money without receiving a service in return. RS reported the matter to the police and attempted to locate the couple but without success.

(vii) On 27 April 2019 concerns were raised by support staff that RS was the subject of financial abuse online by persons he had not met. RS conceded he had paid money in return for pictures relating to his sexual fetish.

(viii) On 15 June 2019 RS informed a support worker that he intended to go to the north of England for a week after messaging a person on Facebook. RS later confirmed that he went with the intention of doing 'adult baby minding' and had done that once.

(ix) On 24 June 2019 RS was the subject of a safeguarding alert arising out of an allegation that he was involved in child sex offences with the male he was staying with in the north of England. RS was arrested but released without charge. The male with whom RS was staying was alleged to have been messaging a 13 year old girl.

(x) On 31 July 2019 RS went to Darwen to stay with a male with whom he had stayed before. He gave support staff details of his whereabouts and returned later having been asked by the man to leave.

Clearly there are activities listed here that would raise some concern regarding the risk RS was placing himself in by engaging in these activities. Nevertheless, one might observe that there are others without autism or learning disabilities who would place themselves at similar risk. It is clear for anyone wishing to briefly explore the nature of dating online that these services do not exist purely for those who wish to engage in a long-term relationship. Many 'hook up' sites exist that provide opportunity for sexual encounters for those who wish to have them. There is a concern with the attitude of the local authority that this would be disproportionate in using RS's learning disabilities to prevent him doing things that are experienced by many without capacity issues.

In considering expert witness commentary on the case, a chartered psychologist, Dr Taylor, stated:

19
The behaviours around the fetish and the related use of the internet and social media are associated with abnormally impulsive behaviour that *may* be a consequence of his learning disability and impairment in his executive brain function, as formulated by the Chartered Psychologist, Dr Taylor. (Emphasis added.)

It is interesting to note that while Dr Taylor started from a position of considering the RS did not have capacity, further discussion with him changed his mind:

23. Within this context, Dr Lawson provided an addendum report dated 24 April 2020 following a further interview with and examination of RS on 10 April 2020. Based on that further information, Dr Lawson revised his opinion to the extent that he concluded that RS also has capacity to make decisions about his contact with others and has capacity to make decisions about accessing the Internet and social media. In his addendum report, with respect to RS's capacity to make decisions concerning contact with others, Dr Lawson stated as follows:
'In my original report I suggested that [RS's] behaviour, rather than what he says that demonstrates an inability to make decisions about contact. However, his reports to me at the second interview suggests that even in situations where this may appear to be so, [RS] is aware of what is going on, as he can recall the details of instances when he, for example, made decisions to meet with men he had recently met online. With my further understanding of him from the second assessment, it is my view now that he makes unwise decisions at those moments rather than his capacity being impaired. The chronology of his history, presented in my first report indicates that he has behaved in similar ways and for many years ... my view as already stated above, is that [RS] understands and can use relevant information about the risk but is making un wise decisions, similar to reckless behaviour that other young adult may show (as per Cobb J in Re Z & Ors [2016] EWCOP – a case I was directed to in the Additional Questions).'

This is particularly interesting to note because it highlights the need to, if possible, discuss the online behaviours with the individual, rather than deciding for ourselves that we know better and if we would not do something anyone who chose to must have some issue of capacity. Cobb rules are blanket applied once again.

This is illustrated again when considering the evidence given by the social worker arguing that RS did not have capacity:

49. For the reasons I have articulated above, nothing in Ms G's evidence is sufficiently cogent to gainsay this conclusion. ... Ms G states that when RS was asked if he knew why professionals were worried about him, RS said yes, because he met a stranger who he didn't know, RS said he could have been 'a rapist, murderer, child molester or paedo'. ... With respect to the men that RS made contact with during April and May 2018, when asked why professionals were worried RS replied that it was because 'he doesn't really know' the men in question ... Whilst Ms G concentrated heavily on the welfare consequences for RS of having contact with men he had contacted via the Internet or social media, as noted, the outcome of the decision made is not relevant to the question of whether the person taking the decision has capacity for the purposes of the Mental Capacity Act 2005.

This is an interesting ruling because it focuses clearly on the rights of the individual and their wish to engage in risky activity and not be prevented from doing so simply because they have a learning difficulty. Clearly there is disquiet from the social worker coming from a genuine welfare concern, but there is also value bias in effect. Perhaps Ms G raised concerns not based upon best interests, but because it was something she was uncomfortable with herself. We have every sympathy with this position, have experienced value biases ourselves many times and have observed them many times further. It is difficult, even in a professional capacity, to take an objective perspective on these issues. Nevertheless, when it comes to matters that are going to cause significant deprivation of liberty for an individual, objectivity is crucial. What is clear from MacDonald J's ruling is that RS could clearly articulate his understanding of the risks associated with his behaviour, and that he undertook such behaviours with full knowledge of the risks. MacDonald J makes specific reference to some of Cobb J's tests in considering this:

50. With respect to the question of using the Internet and social media, once again I am satisfied that that RS is able to understand, retain and can use or weigh relevant information concerning his use of the Internet and social media. During his second interview with Dr Lawson, RS was able to articulate an understanding of the risks of using the Internet and social media. He was aware that he should not post or access offensive material online and retained his awareness of information relating to privacy online and recalled relevant information about sharing. He was aware, for example, that privacy settings do not prevent screenshots being taken and shared more widely. He was clear in his understanding that

others he may meet online may not be who they say they are and that those who appeared to have his interests at heart may not do so. He was able to articulate the risks to himself of using the Internet, including sexual, financial, emotional and/or physical harm.

MacDonald J also observes the value bias that may be present in the local authority's argument that RS did not have capacity:

> 53. Within this context, I accept the evidence of Dr Lawson that, on balance, and having regard to the information made available to Dr Lawson between his substantive and addendum reports, it is not possible to say RS's decision making with respect to contact and the use of the Internet and social media result, as repetitively risky and unwise as it is, results from an impairment in the functioning of his mind and brain, as opposed to from his psychological makeup, his sexual proclivities and desire and the fact he is a young man with a level of impulsivity commonly seen at his age, which factors cause him to make unwise but capacitous decisions (within this context, and as I noted during the course of the hearing, the behaviour of RS in meeting up with strangers after only limited contact with them online, *which the local authority seeks to characterise as so fundamentally irrational that it must demonstrate that RS lacks capacity*, is now also the basis of some widely used social media applications). (Emphasis added.)

Ultimately, MacDonald J stated that RS did have capacity, and the local authority request was rejected.

[2020] EWCOP 32

In this case, presided over by HHJ Richardson, there is much conflict between the wishes of a mother and her view of expert assessment of capacity. While much falls outside of engagement with social media and the internet (for example, capacity to use contraception), there is a specific issue around the mother's wish to demonstrate her daughter does not have capacity to engage with social media, and the 'evidence' she uses to demonstrate this.

The individual whose capacity was being considered was SB, a young woman aged 30 who had been diagnosed with a mild to moderate learning disability. While she lived with her mother during the week, she spent most weekends with her partner CJ.

SB's mother, AB, had previously brought proceedings in the Court of Protection when SB left home to live with a previous partner. When SB returned home voluntarily, AB withdrew the proceedings. AB raises concerns about a previous assessment of SB's capacity to engage with social media, saying she does not understand the risks associated with using them and should therefore not be allowed to access them.

AB says this in relation to social media:

17. AB is concerned that whilst SB was able to state that she understood the risks of social media, SB does not apply her apparent understanding of those risks when actually accessing social media. SB continues to add unknown individuals to her Facebook and to converse with them, providing personal information. Historically, AB reports that SB has met men on social media and determined that they are safe, despite warnings from others around her. AB considers that this behaviour demonstrates a lack of ability to weigh up the relevant information around risk when using social media.

AB argued that the expert assessor had not considered SB's behaviour sufficiently in their assessment:

18. Dr O'Donovan has not, in AB's view, placed sufficient weight on SB's past behaviour and whether she actually understands why that behaviour was unacceptable in the context of social media. An example cited by AB has been that SB has previously posted pictures of her son on social media, however when it was explained to her why these had to be taken down, SB was angry and confused. Dr O'Donovan does not appear to have discussed with SB as to whether she now understands why this was necessary, or whether her understanding of the risks is beyond superficial.

There is a suggestion with the evidence presented by AB that perhaps this is not particularly about SB's capacity to engage with social media, but a wish to control her behaviour when she does something she does not agree with. While we acknowledge we have already done this earlier in the text, it is worthwhile to reiterate and emphasise the point that someone with a learning difficulty who is engaging in social media in a manner that is conducted by many without such difficulties should not be treated differently. There are many millions of social media users who would be hard pressed to give a detailed biography of everyone with whom they are connected on a given platform. Furthermore, one need only watch social media timelines during the *back to school* season at the start of September to see the volume of parents posting images of their children.

However, HHJ Richardson states that AB failed to provide evidence:

58. It is clear from Dr O'Donovan's report that SB is able to understand the risks of social media and weigh them up:

'14.4.3 SB went on to explain that people that she met on social media may not be who they claim to be. She said that such people could mislead her and give her incorrect information. She said that on the basis of her previous experience of meeting others on social media that if she were to accept a friend request from somebody she did not know in the future, she would want to have evidence that they did not have a "Police record".'

59. In her addendum report Dr O'Donovan addressed AB's concerns and concluded, at paragraph 3.9.4 that:

'I therefore do not consider that SB's understanding of the methods and rationale for sharing personal information to be superficial in such a way that this would impact on her ability to use and weigh the relevant information when posting on social media.'

60. There is no proper basis for questioning that conclusion.

Again, this is a clear demonstration of awareness of risks and articulation of how to mitigate those risks. While AB might not be happy with some of SB's online activities, there was no evidence to show that her learning disability was the reason she was doing them and, furthermore, that this demonstrated she was placing herself at a risk of something she did not understand. The request to declare SB lacked capacity to engage with social media was rejected.

[2020] EWCOP 43

This case was a rebuttal to [2020] EWCOP 32, along with a request to conclude proceedings by the Official Solicitor, heard by Anderson HHJ. In this rebuttal AB brought further 'evidence' that SB was at risk and there was a need for further assessment of capacity and potential further/different care. It is interesting to note AB's evidence of this:

16. It is submitted on behalf of AB that SB spends a lot of time communicating with people on social media and that she is very evasive when asked by her mother who she has been communicating with. I note that I have not seen any evidence from AB to this effect. I have not seen any evidence that there is a perceived risk from any specific individual or group of individuals as a result of this pastime. Furthermore, I have been reminded that SB has capacity to access the Internet and social media and is entitled to do so. I accept the submission of the Official Solicitor that it would not be unusual for a 30-year-old woman with capacity to engage in social media to be reluctant to inform her mother about the detail of those communications.

We would agree with the view of the Official Solicitor that not wishing to speak to one's parents about every social media post is not evidence of a lack of capacity. We would suggest should it be a capacitous individual, it might demonstrate someone who understands their right to privacy. Anderson HHJ was not convinced that any new evidence demonstrated lack of capacity and agreed to conclude proceedings in this case.

[2020] EWCOP 66

In this judgment by Keehan J there was concern regarding a 19-year-old male, AA, who had been diagnosed as having autism and Asperger's Syndrome. He has a supported living placement arranged by the local authority. AA has some paraphillic interests, including autoerotic asphyxiation (AEA) and kidnap and rape fantasies. It was noted at the start of the ruling that AA had posted on the dark web about wanting to be a submissive partner who wanted to be kidnapped and raped.

Keehan J was asked to judge on AA's capacity to access the internet and social media, contact with others and consent to sexual relations, as well as AA's best interest where he lacked capacity, and whether to authorise deprivation of liberty.

The salient points of the judgment relating to online services focus on AA's general online behaviour and the relationship between his online life and the potential harm from sexual practices such as AEA. Keehan J noted AA's online activities:

12. In respect of his use of the internet and social media, I note the following:

(i) sexually explicit material has been found on his mobile telephone;
(ii) he has advertised online his desire to be a submissive partner, be kidnapped and raped;
(iii) he has posted graphic sexual content;
(iv) the police had previously found that AA has sent hundreds of explicit messages and photographs to men around the world and asked to be kidnapped;
(v) more recently, since the restrictions on the use of his mobile phone were relaxed, AA has been communicating with another male who shared sexually explicit pictures with AA and they have exchanged texts relating to 'My Little Pony', sexual preferences, submission and depression; and
(vi) AA is sometimes on his mobile phone until 4:00am or 5:00am.

While there are clearly some behaviours listed here that are a cause for concern, the question should be asked about whether these relate to issues of capacity, or age and wish for sexual exploration. Certainly it would not be unusual for someone to discover sexually explicit material on a 19 year-old male's mobile phone. Equally, being on his phone until 4 or 5 am are not unheard of for those of that age, who, perhaps, do not have a regular working routine. While the other points are more of a concern, again, these is nothing to suggest these would be specific to someone with ASD and Asperger's Syndrome.

Keehan J makes it clear in the discussion that it was important to differentiate between social media access (where he agreed that AA had capacity) and sexual rights, specifically to engage in AEA.

In the ruling it was noted how the current care arrangement took place in the placement setting, to ensure AA was *safe*:

> 28. Ms Y spoke of her good working relationship with AA. She told me about the extensive efforts the local authority had made to provide support for AA particularly in relation to his engagement in AEA: all to no avail to date. The current care arrangements and restrictions on AA's liberty are:
>
> (i) one to one staffing at all times with visual checks every 10 minutes throughout the day and every 15 minutes when he is asleep;
> (ii) no unsupervised access in the community or social time;
> (iii) his mobile phone is checked every evening by a member of staff; and
> (iv) his bedroom is searched by the staff twice per day.

However, Keehan J noted that when he met AA, AA was not happy with these restrictions, which he found too invasive:

> 29. When I met with AA prior to the hearing, he was clear that he found these restrictions too invasive and he wished for them to be removed or reduced. Ms Y told me that the current care provider would not be able to maintain the placement if these restrictions were reduced because of the risks of AA harming himself or unintentionally causing his own death. She did accept that the local authority should consider a reduction in the restrictions to give AA some private time and increase his autonomy. If AA engaged in therapeutic support when available, she would then be encouraged to take steps to reduce the support/ restrictions.

Given our own discussions when delivering advice or training, we can again see here some confusion between online access and engaging in AEA. If the concern lay with harm AA might cause to himself from engaging in AEA, we can see the logic in visual checks, but see less justification for mobile device checks, which have implications for AA's privacy. While he might be discussing AEA on his phone, there are many other uses of the device that do not relate to safeguarding concerns, and it is unclear what mobile checks would achieve in monitoring for AEA.

The judgment again makes reference to Cobb J's rules and their application in this case:

> 36. I was referred to the decision of the Court of Appeal in B v Local Authority [2019] EWCA Civ 913 where capacity to engage in the use of social media was in issue. The court approved Cobb J's list of relevant information.
>
> As the Court of Appeal observed, at paragraph 44 of the judgment, this list is only guidance which must be tailored to the individual case. Albeit on the facts of this case, the Official Solicitor submitted that Cobb J's list could be applied to AA without amendment.

However, the comment about Cobb J's list being applied without amendment is an interesting one, given that Cobb J specified the rules he set out were for guidance only, and should not be viewed as definitive test to assess capacity. However, Keehan J is keen to state that the judgment should be based upon AA's capacity as a result of his autism, rather than any subjective unease with hearing of a young man engaging in risky sexual practices or meeting strangers online:

> 46. Capacitous individuals engage in AEA notwithstanding that it is an inherently dangerous practice which carries a very real risk of acquired brain damage or unintentional death. Many capacitous individuals engage in contact with strangers on the internet or on social media which puts, or may put them, at risk of physical, sexual, emotional or psychological harm. They are entitled to make an unwise decision.
>
> 47. I also accept that in approaching the issues in this case I must not adopt an approach based on a moral judgment about AEA or on contacting strangers on the internet or social media. Nor must I adopt a protective stance towards a person when determining whether they have capacity to make a decision to engage in AEA notwithstanding that they are very likely to make an unwise or risky decision.

In reaching a judgment, Keehan J was clear to differentiate between engaging with the internet and social media (for which it was decided AA had capacity) and engagement with AEA, where it was decided AA did not have capacity.

56. In relation to AA's contact with others he meets online, I agree the local authority should draft a care plan for the court's approval.

57. In this case a best interests framework needs to be developed which:

(i) enables the professionals and the court to be better informed about the impact of AA's ASD on his life and his functioning;

(ii) enables the professionals and the court to better understand how AA can be supported to gain capacity to make decisions about these two issues; and

(iii) permits AA sufficient autonomy of decision making and respects his right to a private life whilst balancing the need to protect him from harm.

In addition, it was made clear that a care and support plan must have education as part of the approach, with a focus both on online safety and also positive discussions about sexual gratification. Keehan J also noted that the restrictions currently placed upon AA were very invasive, and perhaps the local authority would reflect upon their appropriateness:

61. AA is subject to very invasive restrictions. At the moment they are necessary to protect him and to ensure his life is not unnecessarily endangered. I would hope that the local authority and the care provider will give anxious consideration to the degree, if at all, to which some of the restrictions may be reduced, pending the outcome of the assessments, education and therapy referred to above. Such reductions if safely achievable will recognise AA's right to a private life and will increase his autonomy.

Overall, we see this as an important judgment that is mindful of safeguarding concerns but also focused very much on individual rights rather than value bias on the part of care professionals.

[2021] EWCOP 20

This case is perhaps the most helpful in considering internet and social media use. In this case, heard by Williams J, a 19-year-old male with autism, EOA, who was removed from his parents' care in 2015 as a result of social care concerns about isolation from society and education, with an extreme religious indoctrination, as well as emotional and physical abuse. In the proceedings the local authority sought final declarations that EOA lacked capacity to make decisions related to:

- foreign travel and holding a passport;
- use of the internet and social media;
- contact.

While obviously a lot of this judgment falls outside of the scope of our interests for this book, there is much consideration regarding capacity to use the internet and social media:

13
(iii) In relation to social media and internet usage the Local Authority's initial position was that they accepted that consideration of his capacity to use social media was distinct from the general consideration of contact. As the case progressed their position developed such that they accepted that the issue should properly be bifurcated to recognise that EOA's general usage of the Internet plainly fell into one domain whereas his ability to contact family members in respect of whom he lacked capacity in the domain of contact fell into another.

17
(iii) Internet and social media access: The Official Solicitor also initially took a similar position to the Local Authority in relation to social media and internet usage. Their position also adapted to recognise that whilst generic issues of internet usage and social media could properly be fitted within the jurisprudence in this field that if one considered the particular decision in relation to use of social media and the Internet in relation to contact with family members it could not properly be distinguished from the issues of EOA's capacity to have contact with them. The Official Solicitor thus submitted that an interim declaration was appropriate in relation to generic Internet and social media issues to enable support to be given to EOA to enable him to make capacitors decisions in this regard by giving him information as to the risks of exploitation by third parties via the Internet. In relation to issues of internet and social media use for the purposes of contact they accepted that a final declaration could properly be made but that it should be made in the domain of contact making specific reference to social media and Internet in that regard.

This is both progressive in scope and focused upon the best interests of EOA. While there were concerns regarding his use of online technology to contact his family, there were many aspects of online use that did not relate to this, and there was no potential for harm arising from the more 'regular' online activities. By acknowledging the difference between general and specific uses of online technology, the judgment does attempt to move conversations around capacity to engage with online services along from a binary choice – it should not simply be that individuals with mental capacity issues can or cannot use online technologies.

In considering expert witness testimony, it was interesting to note that the observation regarding lack of capacity around social media was more one of education than fundamental capacity:

36
Social Media
He understands much related to this field. It seems likely that his current level of social naïveté means that he does not understand the more sophisticated ideas about deception online. However, I think it is likely that he could learn this information with some education and support. I base this on his paranoid and conspiratorial views, which require a similar level of cognitive ability. It is of note that EOA understood some of the benefits of internet use such as connecting with family, shopping online, looking at things that interest him (cars and cartoons). He can also use Skype independently to speak to his brother. Overall, I think that EOA lacks some areas of understanding in relation to the use of the internet. These deficits are a product of his Autism and family circumstances, especially his lack of wider social experience. On this basis EOA lacks capacity with regards to internet and social media use.

Unless capacity for contact is considered to be linked to capacity for internet and social media use in EOA's case, then EOA's capacity for internet and social media is not tied to any contentious or secretive areas. Therefore, it would be relatively easy for him to be given additional education to learn the relevant information.

In his judgment, Williams J continued to make this distinction, and the need to consider each aspect separately:

51. In relation to contact with strangers or third parties it is appropriate to consider the established formulation of the relevant information. Dr Layton identified EOA's lack of understanding of his own vulnerability arising from his lack of social awareness, social naïveté and autism which make him vulnerable to exploitation and abuse. His fixed thinking and unwillingness to consider these issues prevent him weighing issues relating to his vulnerability and he thus lacks capacity to make decisions about contact with strangers. There is an argument that in relation to contact with strangers that EOA might with the provision of information and support capacity to make decisions about contact

with strangers in the way that he might with support regain be able to make capacitous decisions in relation to general social media and Internet use. However, I think there is a distinction. The issues of lack of understanding of his vulnerability and his susceptibility to exploitation by strangers in relation to contact are more profound than those which bear upon social media and Internet usage. There is some link in that one can lead to the other but the progress that EOA would need to make in understanding his vulnerability in face-to-face relationships with third parties or strangers are far more deep rooted and are likely only to be addressed through the three-pronged, long-term care and treatment plan. I am therefore satisfied that EOA lacks capacity in relation to making decisions about contact with strangers and that the final declaration should be made in this regard. I do not consider that an interim declaration is appropriate in this regard.

Williams J makes use of the [2019] EWCOP 2 ruling to provide guidance on making a decision and reiterated the importance of educational intervention modifying the lack of capacity. These elements are quoted in full as there is a lot to unpick with them:

52. I'm satisfied that in relation to general issues of access to the Internet and social media that decisions such as Re A (Capacity: Social media an Internet use: best interests) [2019] EWCOP 2 provide a proper route map to a decision in relation to this issue. The evidence establishes that EOA's capacity to use social media and the Internet is currently hampered by his lack of awareness of the possibility of deception and exploitation by third parties with interests adverse to his own [decision domain 1]. This in Dr Layton's view amounted to a lack of understanding which meant he lacked capacity. Dr Layton's thought he might gain capacity relatively easily with appropriate support and information in this area.

53. However, I am satisfied that this approach does not assist in relation to the particular decision which arises in relation to use of the Internet and social media for the purposes of searching for his family or contacting them. In this regard the issue is far more closely aligned with the approach to contact with other named individuals where the courts evaluation should be decision specific. The use of the Internet or social media is merely one vehicle by which EOA might seek or have contact with family members who pose a risk to him and in respect of whom he lacks capacity to make decisions as to contact. Social media and the Internet today are the modern equivalent of a telephone directory or a letter of a previous era; they are simply a means of gathering information or communicating and in this case where there are clearly identified

individuals whom EOA lacks capacity to make decisions in relation to contact seems to me that this should be recognised. The danger of not dividing these domains into more specific identifiable decisions would be to either apply an approach which was too restrictive in that it would apply a high bar in relation to strangers which in fact was only relevant to family members or alternatively it would apply too low a bar relevant to strangers to issues of contact with high risk family. I am satisfied that the statutory scheme and the jurisprudence does not require such an approach but requires a tailored and decision specific approach where that is appropriate on the facts.

Williams J goes further in this paragraph, separating the use of the internet and social media in general as one decision on capacity, then another regarding capacity to use the internet and social media for contact with AA's family. This is a very important distinction to be made in a ruling, and breaks away from our already remarked concerns that 'internet and social media' is too broad a term when considering best interests and deprivation of liberty:

Thus, the order in relation to general internet and social media use should be an interim order which reflects the fact that further practicable steps to enable EOA to make capacious decisions in this regard. In relation to social media and Internet usage in the context of contact with family members that should be incorporated in the declarations addressing contact.

Therefore, in his conclusions Williams J stated:

63. I will therefore make declarations that EOA lacks capacity to make decisions in relation to;

(i) Foreign travel.
(ii) Contact with his family and others.
(iii) Social media and Internet usage.

64. In relation to social media and Internet usage this will be an interim declaration.
65. I determine that it is in EOA's best interests for the care support and treatment plan to be implemented. The care and support plan needs to be amended and the treatment plan needs to be set out in black-and-white following the professionals meeting.

As we have stated earlier, this is a very important judgment when considering how to support an individual with potential capacity issues around engaging with the internet and social media. It should not be a yes or no decision: it should consider the nature of the use of online technology and where the harms exist; and then whether education would help improve capacity; before putting restrictions in place that would support an individual at risk of harm, without depriving them of access to other aspects of online activity that bear no risk.

Implications

This and the preceding chapter provide a detailed exploration of how the law and Court of Protection proceedings are applied around what we might broadly call adult online safeguarding. While it is a comprehensive examination, we feel this is extremely important, because the Court of Protection is ultimately where deprivation of liberty can occur and individuals can have access to social media or the internet withdrawn. By exploring the different proceedings that relate to capacity to engage with online services, it also allowed a detailed exploration of the complexity of cases, the challenges of making judgements on these issues and also the evidence that is brought to bear to justify the wishes of care teams and parents in doing something that will deprive an individual of what is described by some as a fundamental human right.

While the original Cobb J rulings that laid the foundations for capacity to access the internet and social media seem to have established the term in Court of Protection proceedings, it is important also to note that Cobb J made reference to having to build these rulings, and the increasingly ubiquitous tests, from a shallow foundation. The Court of Appeal ruling referring to [2019] EWCOP 3 makes particular mention, with which we would agree, that the list specified by Cobb J is a useful tool as long as it is treated as guidance, rather than a definitive test. It is important, in the view of the Court of Appeal, that the tests are applied based upon the specific needs of a particular case.

> 67. So far as concerns the appropriateness of the list, as in the case of the list specified by Cobb J in relation to a decision to use social media, we see no principled problem with the list provided that it is treated and applied as no more than guidance to be expanded or contracted or otherwise adapted to the facts of the particular case.

It is therefore important, when considering subsequent Court of Protection rulings, to consider whether this advice is being heeded. We have seen, in this detailed exploration of rulings, that the 'Cobb rules' are indeed being considered, sometimes as a starting point for consideration and sometimes in their entirety. It is encouraging to see later rulings, such as, in our view, the crucially important [2021] EWCOP 20, that the concept of the 'internet and social media' is being diversified to consider the particular aspect of online behaviour that is causing concern, which raises the important distinction to isolate just these behaviours. While it is, arguably, easier for those with caring responsibilities to simply remove devices and internet access, if an individual is engaged in some practice online that places them at risk, it would rarely be in the best interests of an individual to do this. Let us consider a hypothetical scenario where an individual, CC, an 18-year-old male with a mild learning disability, uses online technology to engage in two different practices:

1. CC makes use of online gaming platforms to play multi-player video games, he is part of a gamer clan and considers the members of this clan to be his friends. CC's care team make no note that this online gaming places him at any risk, and there are many positives to take from this activity.
2. He in engaged with discussion groups on discussion boards (for example, 4chan) where there is much anti-Semitic activity and CC is encouraged to post up anti-Semitic images and comments. CC has never received any education around online hate speech or the personal risks in posting this material.

If a Court of Protection judgment or care provider simply concluded that because of activity 2, and CC's lack of appreciation of the potential risk in engaging in hate speech (as a result of never having received education about it), he fails to have capacity to engage with the internet and social media, they are also removing his access to a positive, innocuous activity from which he gains much enjoyment. A more progressive approach would be to consider an education package to get CC to understand online hate speech and, if the behaviour persists, look at restricting access to certain websites to limit opportunity to engage in such discourse.

Furthermore, the interchange between the internet and social media is problematic – the internet is the underpinning technology to provide the majority of forms of digital communication. It is, in a most basic definition, simply a collection of connected computer networks which use common communication protocols to allow applications to interact with each other. Social media is simply a class of these applications – allowing person-to-person contact and interaction between remote devices accessing information hosted on large systems making use of the internet to enable the technical communication. While it may seem that we are splitting technical semantics here, it is important to understand the distinction. Referring to 'the internet and social media' is both too generic and too restrictive – it fails to encompass other areas of digital communication, such as messaging, gaming or streaming content.

We have also seen, through different Court of Protection rulings, that care team and even expert assessors might bring their own value biases to proceedings. While a care team might be uncomfortable with an individual engaging in AEA, or contacting strangers online for casual sex, there should not be a call for proceedings for what a care team might consider to be *risky* without evidence of risk. Risk perceptions are subjective (Beck, 1992). We have also seen parental attempts at intervention, or withdrawal of access, for little more reason than a perceived loss of control by the parent. While, in this case, the judgment made clear that the individual did have capacity, the fact it required a Court of Protection proceeding to rule on that is concerning: surely this was a case for counselling by the care team or mediation, rather than formal judgment? What is clear from this detailed exploration of rulings is that this is an area that is exploring the knowledge base and trying to interpret digital risk while still learning about it. One of the key arguments from this book is that while there is much to learn from the lessons on child online safeguarding, there are many pitfalls to avoid too. One of this is certainly what we have already referred to as digital unconscious bias, which can be framed as bringing one's own personal online experiences into professional settings and making supposedly objective decisions as a result. Clearly this is a concern when were are talking about decisions that can impact significantly on a vulnerable person's liberty. In the next chapter we explore this phenomenon in more detail, drawing upon empirical data from our experiences in providing advice, and delivering training, for various care professionals.

5

The safeguarding dystopia

Introduction

In the previous two chapters we conducted an extensive review of the legal perspectives on capacity to access the internet and social media and how Court of Protection proceedings have developed since the [2019] EWCOP 2 and [2019] EWCOP 3 rulings, specifically Cobb J's tests for capacity. Through this exploration, with a focus on the best interests of the individual, it is clearly evident that there are both positive and negative aspects of the rulings. There are a number of key findings from this analysis:

- **Generic concept of 'internet and social media' as a catch all** – prior to [2019] EWCOP 20 very little distinction was made between different online activities, it was merely where an individual had capacity to engage with the internet and social media. This is far too broad a term if we are considering whether someone has capacity, and a conclusion that someone does not have capacity for a specific aspect (for example being unable to appreciate the deception of 'friends' on social media) should not mean that any online access is barred. Withdrawal of the right to engage with digital technology has significant impact on liberty and the individual's human rights, and removal of access to all aspects of digital life, as a result of risk-taking behaviour in one aspect, seems highly disproportionate.
- **The application of the tests in absolute terms and a higher bar for individuals with capacity issues** – even though Cobb J has stated that the tests he defined were guidance only, to be adapted to the specifics of a given case, there is evidence that in some cases it is being applied literally. We also see evidence of aspects of the test being used to set a bar higher for someone with capacity issues compared to someone without. There are many people without learning difficulties who would struggle to articulate how to keep their social media accounts safe, or are happy to share their login details with others. These behaviours should not be used as a reason to suggest that an individual does not have capacity.
- **Knowledge of experts** – it is apparent through a number of rulings and, indeed, acknowledged by Cobb J in his original judgments, that this is not an area where the Court of Protection has a great deal of knowledge. There is, therefore, a reliance upon expert testimony to make the case either for or against capacity to engage with internet and social media.

We have identified a number of instances in these proceedings where expert statements could be found lacking – whether by being inaccurate about the law, bringing value biases to proceedings (identified explicitly by MacDonald J in [2020] EWCOP 29) or making claims of behaviour that relates to an individual's disability that are clearly untrue (for example having explicit content on their phone or staying up into the early hours engaged in online activities).

- **Interventions to control** – there has been evidence of excessive control in some aspects of proceedings, such as demands to spot-check devices, widespread access control, and monitoring of access. In some of these cases it was not clear what this intervention would achieve; there was certainly no evidence that spot-checking a device would result in an individual being free from risk or harm as a result.

In conducting this analysis, the conclusion we reach is not that this is done for any malicious reason; rather it is as a result of the aforementioned value biases, or *digital unconscious bias*, by those wishing to do their best for the individuals in their care, but reacting to behaviours they actually perhaps do not understand or engage with themselves, so will tend toward a poorly informed response to deal with any presented risk. We can see, for example, that if a professional had concerns about an individual accessing illegal content online, which could result in arrest and incarceration, they might decide that the best way to mitigate this risk would be to impose a spot-checking regime so that they can see what the individual is looking at and whether there is cause for concern. However, what the professional fails to appreciate is that this is also a serious invasion of the individual's privacy (given that one's mobile device is a window into their social life, interests and beliefs). While the discovery of access to inappropriate material may result in the professional feeling justified in their approach, we would seriously question whether this is the best approach.

We have seen in the proceedings, and also our own work with professionals, that there is frequently a belief that technology can provide a useful solution to what is considered to be a problem *caused by technology*. We have already mentioned Ranum's Law in Chapter 2, which is well established among technology regulation thinkers, however much of it is ignored by government. We can see within the draft Online Safety Bill once again the view that providers can put some magic technology in place to eradicate any social ill that exists on their system.

At the time of writing, we are in the midst of yet another debate around the responsibility of technology providers to tackle social challenges. After the European Football Championship Final in July 2021, where England were beaten on penalties by Italy, social media became a channel for racial hate, where black English footballers were targeted with racial abuse.

The predicable fallout from this was, as is always the case when digital communication is used to abuse, the technology itself is to blame, and the assumption is that it must always provide the solution. Questions to politicians around the racist abuse of footballers on social media have consistently been met with "this is unacceptable, and the Online Safety Bill will address it". As already mentioned, at the core of the Draft Online Safety Bill is a *duty of care* for providers to demonstrate they have considered the risks and harms that could arise if someone used their platform, and to provide evidence that in the event of harmful content, they will move to remove it. It therefore proffers the view, once more, that technology should tackle this.

However, if we consider the issues regarding algorithmically tackling racist discourse online, there are a number of problems. A filtering approach, as described in Chapter 2, will generally be based upon keyword-based interventions. While there are some words used in racist discourse that are clearly identifiable as racist, there are others, such as those associating people with primates, or certain types of fruit, that are less straightforward to capture through an algorithm immediately as racist. While there can be some coded solutions that attempt to place context around the statement (for example, a word directed at an individual, the use of swear words alongside the potentially racist terms), it is very difficult for an algorithm to detect it automatically and to have a high success rate. And there are potential litigation risks in a platform accusing a user of being a racist when the context of their post, misunderstood by their algorithms, turns out to be nothing of the sort.

It is interesting to note that, in all of the current media debate around these issues, most fail to mention that platforms provide tools to report offensive posts, which will then be looked at by a moderator to determine whether they fail *community standards*. While community standards vary between platforms, they are generally below legal thresholds and provide the means to alert the platform to abusive and harmful content and comments. In general, in these cases, if there is clear evidence of hate speech, a platform will remove an account or, at the very least, suspend it. This is more holistic in approach in that the community is self-managing the behaviour of its members and policing itself; it does highlight that tools are available, should individuals care to look. The fact that bystanderism is the default position of politicians, with an assumption that magic algorithms can address these issues without intervention, highlights the zeitgeist of 'someone needs to do something' while not doing anything themselves.

Therefore, professionals should be forgiven for assuming the same. If those who govern us assume that this can all be sorted out without having to tackle the core social issues (which, one would suggest, existed in a pre-internet world) why would those whose exposure to the digital world has solely been personal and social, but are now being expected to make professional judgements in the best interests of others, think any differently? This chapter considers the need for detailed knowledge in supporting those who are vulnerable and at risk of online harm, and the need for critical discourse in professional approaches. As we have already stated in this book, we do not intend this to be a *how to* textbook, more a discussion of the critical issues in the online safeguarding of vulnerable adults and how they are best responded to by stakeholders (see Chapter 7).

The first part of this chapter considers in more detail the sources of professionals' knowledge, knowledge gaps, and how we might move towards a more objective, knowledge-informed approach to judgements on individuals' capacity issues and how individuals might be better supported to have a full, risk-mitigated digital life. As such, in this chapter we argue that the essence of online safeguarding practice is flawed in its isolationist approach, both in that failing to understand online behaviours may only reach a harmful threshold as a result of wider acts, and that a mitigation approach that essentially looks to block or withdraw online access fails to appreciate the social dimensions of the potential for abuse. We also return to the topic of technological intervention (introduced in Chapter 2), the reliance on technology and the reality of its capabilities, arguing that without effective knowledge, it is too often employed to *enforce* safeguarding, with little consideration of capabilities of the technology or its impact upon the rights of the individual(s) it is being applied to/imposed upon. Indeed, some of the empirical data we draw upon from our exploration of professionals' knowledge around the online safeguarding of vulnerable adults specifically calls for this. We also draw upon examples of excess use of technology, and the potential motivations for this. This will, we would hope, present a stronger case for what technology can and cannot do, and it will also highlight how technology can be used, against a safeguarding backdrop, as controlling rather than supportive.

'This has not been an issue for us to date'

As we have already emphasised, there is a concern in our work that where national policy seems to imply *someone else* has to ensure online safety for individuals at risk of harm, and that someone is generally the technology provider, we cannot express surprise when social care professionals adopt such policy discourses and express similar views. We have met many excellent, well-qualified and experienced professionals who are working extremely hard to do their best for the individuals in their care. However, few, if any, have actually received any training on digital issues. One need only listen to media discussions and debates around online safeguarding to see that opinion is often presented as fact. In Prime Minister's Questions on 14 July 2021, Boris Johnson, when challenged on addressing online racial abuse, said, regarding social media platforms (Johnson, 2021), '[u]nless they get hate and racism off their platforms, they will face fines amounting to 10% of their global revenues. We all know they have the technology to do it.'

We have already discussed earlier how challenging it is to implement an algorithm to identify racist content while avoiding that which is not. The platforms certainly do not have the technology to do this, which is why the proposed legislation from the Online Safety Bill relies on demonstration of risk assessment and due diligence, rather than an absolute duty of platforms to guarantee their services are free from harmful content.

In practice, assumed knowledge arises from personal use, which is then applied to professional settings. It is a perennial challenge when considering how to develop one's professional knowledge regarding digital technology that because its use is as a social activity, and potentially also within the professional setting to support working practices, there is an assumption that we will *absorb* knowledge about it (as if by osmosis), or simply apply our own views on its use to the professional setting. Of course, this is not an effective way to develop sound knowledge in a profession context and brings unconscious biases and value judgements that are not based in objectivity. While training for online safety in the children and young people's workforce is relatively well established, with statutory duties of schools defined, there is still much to be achieved (UK Safer Internet Centre, 2020). In all the training sessions we have delivered to date, we have yet to meet a professional (whether statutory or non-statutory) who has received formal training on digital issues for safeguarding adults before they attended the event. It has been clear in all sessions that professionals had been working with individuals about their use of digital technology. We cannot emphasise enough that making personal use of social media, group chats and online shopping does not mean one is sufficiently knowledgeable to make important safeguarding judgements regarding online risk and an individual's liberty.

The quote in the title of this section is taken from a response to a Freedom of Information (FOI) request to a local authority, where we wished to determine whether their social care professionals had been updated on proceedings from the Court of Protection since [2019] EWCOP 2 and [2019] EWCOP 3. Specifically we asked: 'Since the Court of Protection decisions in Re A (Capacity: Social Media and Internet Use: Best Interests) [2019] EWCOP 2 and Re B (Capacity: Social Media: Care and Contact) [2019] EWCOP 3, what education and/or guidance have you delivered/ developed for your Adult Social Care workforce?' The response we received was: 'No guidance has been developed – this has not been an issue for us to date. We will review the need for this guidance should the requirement arise.'

We quote this response here because it gives us a chance to reflect upon our own concerns regarding professional responses to supporting vulnerable adults in the online space. It would seem from the local authority's response that it is taking a *reactive* view in that it will consider the rulings only should any issue related to someone in its care become at risk from online harms and be reported to them. We would counter that, surely, any local authority with caring responsibilities needs to be proactive in considering response, unless there is no means for individuals to engage with online services within the local authority geographic area. The case we make through this discussion is that there is a dearth of expectation across the social care sector that this is an area that requires any formal training and professional development. It is interesting that while the mantra of 'safeguarding is everyone's responsibility' and the importance of adopting a coordinated approach through multi-agency working has been subsumed into numerous policies and guidance both nationally and regionally, this fundamental principle seems to have been forgotten in translation to digital. This is, as we have discussed earlier, reflective of a national perspective that online harms should be tackled by the providers of platforms upon which these harms take place. We have gone to great lengths throughout this book to present a counter-argument, namely, technology cannot be the sole solution to online harms, and, as with most safeguarding decisions, input is required from many stakeholders. If certain stakeholders lack knowledge of harms and the underlying environments upon which they manifest, they will not be equipped to support those who need care.

We previously outlined in Chapter 2 the trajectory of online safeguarding children and young people and one term we have come across frequently in the last two decades is *digital native*. Coined by Prensky (2001) as a phrase differentiating between children − digital natives − and adults − digital immigrants − the concept rapidly found into way into academic and educational discourse. For example, as one professional observed, "'Oh,' we are told, 'they know more than me because they're a digital native, it just comes naturally to them'."

Prensky's digital native idea comes from an article that proposes a theory where because someone was born in an era where digital technology was ubiquitous, they had some innate ability to engage with it with capabilities that are missing from previous generations generalised as digital immigrants. While this crude generalisation is now widely debunked (Helsper and Eynon, 2010), its use still pervades in popular discourse and we have certainly attended seminars and workshops around digital literacies and safeguarding where senior speakers from government and from regulators have unhelpfully spoken of younger generations being natives capable of navigating the digital world without further support. The term has thus become a taken-for-granted assumption and we frequently hear it from all manner of professionals, mainly used in one of two ways − first, as a way to imply blame: "They're digital natives, they should know about this sort of thing"; or secondly to deflect responsibility: "I'm not a digital native like they are, they know more than me."

Brown and Czerniewicz (2010), among others, are also highly critical of the concept as such terminology hides inequalities in digital experiences and we should instead be concerning ourselves with *digital democracy* – a point we consider highly important to the arguments we present in this book. Furthermore, given that *digital native* ties in with the concept of *Millennials* (born between the mid 1980s and early 2000s) and *Generation Z* (late 1990s–approximately 2015) this is not a term that is simply applied to children and young people now. Many adults would now be considered digital natives if we were to engage with this narrative, but we suggest this is a term that should not have any place in any professional discourse around online safeguarding.

If we return to the three case examples we presented in Chapter 3, we can see in all cases a lack of knowledge resulting in problematic safeguarding decisions:

- concern of harm to an individual in independent but supported living – place them under surveillance and grossly invade their privacy;
- concern regarding an adult with learning difficulties accessing pornography – make it difficult for him to access pornography at home, with the outcome being he visits public places to do so instead;
- concern regarding harm arising from accessing online services on mobile devices – spot-check mobile phones to make sure residents are safe.

We would propose in all of these scenarios that the approach used was taken with the best of intentions, but without the professionals involved having the appropriate knowledge to understand why the decisions made were not in the best interests of the individuals being supported.

We have also reflected upon our own empirical work giving professional training and being involved in policy discussions around supporting adults with potential capacity issues. We have also undertaken research drawing upon observations from these sessions and will consider them in more depth later. As part of study (which had ethical approval from the authors' affiliated university) we also conducted a survey with adult social care professionals and focus group discussions. The goal of this research endeavour was to better understand the knowledge base among professionals with safeguarding responsibilities for vulnerable adults. With the help of a local authority, we undertook the study to get an understanding of the knowledge of professionals in two geographic areas, their training experiences and their perceived needs around online safeguarding. While, as with any study of this nature, we give the caveat that while the respondents were from a wide range of roles in the care professions, and we received 156 responses to the survey, we are not generalising from these responses nor claiming that this is a representative picture of the care sector as a whole, but more of a snapshot of professionals' experiences and attitudes in a field where little research has been done. Nevertheless, it provides us with a useful picture of confidence, knowledge and needs, and does little to conflict with our empirical findings from the training sessions we have conducted with professionals ourselves.

The survey respondents were wide-ranging in post, including social workers, psychiatrists, police, support workers, therapists and managers. It was interesting to note, given this survey took place in 2019, pre-pandemic, while the [2019] and [2019] EWCOP 3 rulings were still very much in the public awareness around adult safeguarding, that we did struggle to recruit respondents. It would seem, reflecting on feedback when trying to collect responses from the subsequent focus group data, that some professionals:

- did not see why this survey would be relevant to their role;
- had not had to support anyone regarding online safeguarding issues so did not see any need to do the survey;
- were so busy/overloaded they did not have time to do the survey, although they did take the time to respond to say they felt it was important;
- felt that as they had done *some* training, they did not need to respond.

Nevertheless, the response rate was sufficient that it allowed us to get a good cross-section of responses and allowed us to explore knowledge and attitudes. The first part of the survey considered whether the respondent had ever been required to support someone with a learning disability or autistic spectrum disorder to access the internet and social media. Just over half of repsondents (53.9 per cent) said that they had – clearly this was not an unusual part of our respondents' roles. In terms of how the people they supported accessed the online world, there were few surprises from the responses (see Table 5.1).

This is very much what we would expect, with the majority of people having personal devices they use to access online services, and also using

Table 5.1: Survey responses of how people the professionals supported accessed the online world

Using family- or provider services (including day services/supported living or residential services)-owned computer or smart device (mobile phones, iPads, tablet, etc)	63.29%
Using their own smart devices (mobile phones, iPad, tablet, etc)	88.61%
Using their own laptop or computer	56.96%
Playing computer games online (Nintendo Switch, Xbox, Play Station, etc)	55.70%
Using local library computers	26.58%

Source: Authors

more communal devices and gaming consoles. We also asked whether respondents had encountered a person with a learning disability or autistic spectrum disorder who had been a victim of online abuse. Again, we were unsurprised to see that just over 43 per cent of respondents said that they had, with 47.5 per cent saying that they had not, and 9 per cent saying they did not know. So, again, clearly it was not unusual for respondents to be involved in helping people who had been victims of online abuse, and to have to support them in some way.

We also asked if they had encountered a person with a learning disability or autistic spectrum disorder who had been a perpetrator of illegal behaviour online. We feel this is a very important question given the potential risk associated with people without capacity engaging in illegal behaviour, highlighted in many of the Court of Protection proceedings explored in Chapters 3 and 4. While the number of respondents who had (35 per cent) was lower than those who had encountered victims of online abuse, it was certainly a significant minority who had experience of this. Fifty-five per cent of respondents said that this was not something they had encountered and a further 10 per cent said they did not know.

It was, therefore, unsurprising that the majority of respondents (57 per cent) said that they had supported a person with a learning disability or autistic spectrum disorder who had encountered online risk. When asked to describe the support that had been offered, and the types of risks encountered, the responses were wide-ranging. Typical responses included:

- Engaging with strangers online, or want to make *friends* online.
- Exchanging intimate images online with friends or strangers.
- People wishing to meet *friends* they had met online and, in some cases, doing so.
- Providing education around online harms and differentiating between real friends and online friends.
- Managing individuals' online privacy.
- Online connections moving to sexual relationships.
- General issues of cyberbullying and abuse.
- Financial exploitation and coercion.
- Making capacity assessment for individuals considered at risk of harm online.

What is clear from the qualitative responses and disclosures in the survey was that there were very few straightforward scenarios. Professionals are dealing with complex cases and needing to make safeguarding judgements are based on rights and best interests. The following examples drawn from the responses illustrate these complexities:

'I noticed that a lady was asking people for sex on her facebook page, she was also sharing her address openly. Some of her "friends" were fetishists. I warned her of the dangers of doing this and asked her not to do it. She was unable to protect herself, but family helped her and tightened up her privacy settings. NB, her sister had set up her facebook account so that she could only add friends of friends, however, one of her contacts with LD was friends online with some dodgy people, and in that way they gained access to her. He was later convicted for paedophilia.'

'I was unaware at the time that they were taking the risk. They were attempting to contact young females through facebook. Police picked up, supported with police, referred to safesurfing project run via mencap.'

'Service users accessing pornographic gambling sites in which they were asked to remove clothes when losing a bet. Referred to Social workers and nursing for support in staying safe online as well as discussing this in therapy session. Service users had capacity for unwise decisions but further education felt to be helpful as well as more activities offered in the evenings.'

'I provided reassurance surrounding their obsessive internet use, in that I attempted to divert their attentions to more productive modes of communication and urged them to understand that they should share any difficulties they found themselves in online with a family member or member of staff. I worked to devise a safe way to access social media, with oversight from staff and family members where appropriate, limiting use and providing training / education where practical surrounding safety and reporting abuse. There has only been support provided to make social media accounts private and not visible to others who may intend to cause them harm.'

'I advised a man with high functioning autism and mild LD in collaboration with the sexual health counsellor on how to develop a healthy relationship with a woman; this was following a safeguarding concern where he was financially exploited by a woman he met in an on-line chat room and she took money of him after meeting up with him. He did not realize this was an escort and thought she was his girlfriend.'

Clearly, none of these cases are simple with easy answers. They require a deep understanding of the issues, the potential risks and how to ameliorate them, and how to effectively support individuals.

We also asked respondents how they would rate their knowledge and understanding of how a person with a learning disability or autistic spectrum disorder may be at risk online and saw a population who were, in general, confident in their knowledge (Table 5.2).

Table 5.2: Survey responses of professionals' knowledge and understanding of online risk

I have an excellent knowledge and understanding	I have a good knowledge and understanding	I have some knowledge and understanding	I have a little knowledge and understanding	I have no knowledge and understanding
5.34%	54.20%	35.88%	4.58%	0.00%

Source: Authors

Table 5.3: Survey responses of professionals' confidence in addressing online risk

Extremely confident	Very confident	Somewhat confident	Not very confident	Not confident at all
5.47%	29.69%	52.34%	11.72%	0.78%

Source: Authors

Table 5.4: Survey responses of professionals' confidence in recognising illegal content online

Extremely confident	Very confident	Somewhat confident	Not very confident	Not confident at all
7.94%	42.06%	38.10%	11.90%	0.00%

Source: Authors

They were similarly confident, albeit slightly less so, in how they might address online risk with the people they support (Table 5.3).

And our respondents were also confident in recognising the difference between illegal and legal content online (Table 5.4).

Therefore, it was no surprise to see, in general, our respondents felt confident in supporting people they worked with in remaining safe online (Table 5.5).

However, perhaps more telling was when respondents were asked whether they had ever received any training or information on online safety. Only 21 per cent of our respondents said that they had. Furthermore, of those who had received training or accessed information, only 53 per cent said this was related to supporting people with learning disabilities and/or autistic spectrum disorders. Therefore, we have quite a confused picture: on the one hand the majority of respondents say that they are confident in dealing, professionally, with supporting the people they worked with in being safe online, whereas only approximately 21 per cent of respondents had ever received any relevant training on the subject.

Table 5.5: Survey responses of professionals' confidence in supporting people in remaining safe online

Extremely confident	Very confident	Somewhat confident	Not very confident	Not confident at all
5.38%	21.54%	60.00%	13.08%	0.00%

Source: Authors

Table 5.6: Comparison of survey responses between professionals who had received training and those who had not

	I have an excellent knowledge and understanding	I have a good knowledge and understanding	I have some knowledge and understanding	I have a little knowledge and understanding	I have no knowledge and understanding
Trained	5.88%	45.58%	39.7%	4.41%	4.41%
Untrained	6.84%	20.83%	56.94%	15.28%	0

Source: Authors

While those who were trained were generally slightly more confident than those who were not, the differences were not great. For example, when comparing the claimed knowledge of those who have, and have not, been trained, there are not too many differences (Table 5.6).

When asked to describe the sort of training that respondents had received, the majority (31/51) said that it was e-learning (that is, an online course). While few elaborated further than simply saying it was a form of e-learning, this immediately raises concerns as two things that are very important when learning about individual responses to specific needs are discussion and being able to ask questions, neither of which are possible in the majority of e-learning scenarios. For those who said they had received different forms of training, the descriptions were wide-ranging, including:

- cybersecurity;
- data protection handling;
- fire safety;
- IT training;
- CEOP ambassadors training (which is in relation to safeguarding children and young people).

Of all the respondents who described their training, only two described either discussion groups or case study analysis – both of which are very important when developing knowledge in this area (Bond and Dogaru, 2019).

When asked how training might be improved, or what they would like training to be like, this became evident, with comments such as:

'Training on identifying specific risks. How to explain risks as simply as possible. How to assess mental capacity in this area and making best interests decisions.'

'Case examples of how practitioners have enabled people to stay safer online – realistic examples within resources available with evidence of the impact that this had.'

'I would like training in this area and updates as the online world is very sophisticated and for ever changing eg new scams that would be useful to be aware of so we can support clients more effectively to enable them to stay safe.'

'My main concern with more complex and novel instances of capacity is at what time as a provider would it be considered to be an expanded test for capacity and if that would be determined as an impermissible attempt to raise the bar, in that to fully understand internet safety, they would need to have a founding knowledge of criminal law.'

Many others referred to the need to understand the law and terminology more effectively, while some called for resources they could also share with people they are working with. It was clear from this list of requirements that many saw the complexity of the area and the need for more effective training. However, there was one comment that was an interesting reflection on the attitude of the FOI respondent at the start of this section: "I've done all the training. We are all up to date on this." This was from a respondent who had never had to deal with an online safeguarding case but was very confident that they had the knowledge to do so, yet described their training experience to date as "[w]e've been doing e-learning online, eg Fire safety training."

Thus we are left with a conundrum. On the one hand we have evidence of many professionals having to tackle online safeguarding issues with vulnerable individuals they work with. The examples given by many were complex in nature. Equally we see the majority saying they are confident in the support they can give and their knowledge of online safeguarding issues. However, only the minority had received training, and in the case of those who had, it was generally an online learning package, rather than detailed interactive training. We are therefore left wondering whether this is a case of not knowing enough to know how little one knows. As the majority of respondents had not received training we must assume that their knowledge, given most think they have *some* knowledge in this area, raises much concern. Exploring the disclosed cases professionals have worked on highlights the need for critical thinking, understanding of the law, the nature of online harms and the best interests of individuals. We fear this is not something that can be developed through one's own use of social media or informal discussions about these issues.

Our hypothesis about how lack of knowledge leads to not appreciating the complexities of the area are further illustrated in training we have delivered in professional settings. We have delivered many training sessions to professionals in varying roles who have safeguarding responsibilities. In general, this training is case based, discursive and multi-disciplinary in nature, with pre-sessional materials that cover key aspects, therefore leaving plenty of opportunity for discussion in the training sessions themselves. One of the key observations from these sessions is lots of confessions of 'I didn't realise how little I knew'. What is clear from case discussions is that is it often viewed as easier to withdraw access than navigate the issues. In one case we often use, we speak of suspicion that an individual the trainees are working with is accessing illegal material on their mobile phone. Most are of the view that they would demand access to the device to check for themselves. Fewer consider discussion or educational intervention so the individual might better understand the risks they are being exposed to as a result of these potential activities. We stress that for police access to a device under section 49 of the Regulation of Investigatory Powers Act 2000 (UK Government, 2000), there is the following requirement:

A disclosure requirement in respect of any protected information is necessary on grounds falling within this subsection if it is necessary—

(a) in the interests of national security;
(b) for the purpose of preventing or detecting crime; or
(c) in the interests of the economic well-being of the United Kingdom.

Therefore, a care professional demanding access without such evidence would be at risk of illegal access themselves. There does seem to be, among these discussions, a wish that 'something' can be done to prevent access, or to mitigate risk by withdrawing technology. We are certainly sympathetic to this viewpoint; however, as we will explore later, this reliance on technology can lead to further rights and legal challenges and rarely provides an effective solution. Furthermore, if presented in a case-based scenario, one starts to identify an overspill from safeguarding concern to punitive control.

We have had many discussions where professionals express fear in relation to adopting a less punitive approach. In one instance a professional said that they had been asked by someone they were working with – a 16-year-old female with autism – about how to access pornography. We expressed the view that perhaps the best approach to that is to counsel them on pornography compared to real sex, the legalities of accessing such content (and we stress that a minor accessing pornography is not breaking any laws), how to disclose if they see anything upsetting, and also to stay on mainstream pornography sites where content is verified and not likely to be extreme or illegal. However, the response of the professional was that, given the parents monitor their child's internet access, they would see she had been looking at pornography, which would place the professional at risk of complaint from the family. Their view was that it was better, professionally, for them if they told the individual not to access pornography. When we point out that if she knew her parents were monitoring her internet access there is a higher likelihood she would, instead of using mainstream sites, move to dark web sites where there was less chance of detection, but more chance of accessing illegal content, the professional agreed, but still said it was not worth the professional risk. What, essentially, was discussed was placing the individual at greater risk of harm because it was considered too risky professionally to support this young person. We have every sympathy with the professional in this instance and have concerns that they felt their employer (a local authority) would not support them in the event of a complaint, which does, we feel, highlight institutional naivety around online safeguarding.

We have also encountered many professionals who feel what we are saying is too progressive or would be ineffective in practice (even though they have never considered a more progressive approach before). It comes as no surprise that, given the lack of training around online safeguarding, professionals instead bring strongly held opinions on these matters, and we frequently hear things like "well, I don't agree with them looking at porn"; "we need to know what they're doing to keep them safe"; or even "it's better if they don't go online". None of these, we fear, would ever be in the best interests of the individual who is perceived to be at risk of harm.

Technical 'solutions'

We have mentioned our many discussions with professionals looking for a technical *solution* to the safeguarding concerns they have. Equally, we have illustrated that this is hardly a surprise given policy narratives around online harms requiring online solutions. Furthermore, we have seen in the survey responses professionals asking for training around how to use technology to keep those they support *safe*. Examples included: "The law in relation to putting protection such as parental controls in place for people over 18. Assume that this can be done in best interests if they lack capacity to make decisions about internet safety"; and "How to switch on privacy settings and what filters are available."

We have, in Chapter 2, started to explore the use of technical interventions to prevent access to online harms. As we discussed in that chapter, there is a rich history of policy assumptions that lead to views the technology can be a good way to address these risks. However, there has clearly been an assumption that technology can provide *the solution* for harm prevention, and this thinking, consequently, results in an overreliance on technology in safeguarding decisions. Why worry about the great complexity, for example, of an educational intervention, if we can put some technology in place that can prevent harm from occurring? In our work across the safeguarding sector, one of the key challenges we face is in overcoming technological determinism in trying to articulate a balanced approach to technological intervention – while there are software packages that can help in safeguarding resolutions, they rarely, if ever, provide a complete solution.

Furthermore, there is a risk, given the somewhat blunt nature of a lot of software solutions, that the nuance often required in such an intervention is lost – we may, for example, wish to filter access to pornographic content. As we have already discussed, there are many pieces of software that offer this service. However, their nature results in the *overblocking* of content that might not be pornographic in nature but makes use of sexual keywords, for example access to information sites on sex, relationships and gender. Is the restriction of access to information that might be extremely valuable to the individual a reasonable consequence of preventing access to pornography?

At the time of writing, the Blocked project, run by the Open Rights Group (see www.blocked.org.uk), which scans URLs against ISP filters to determine levels of overblocking, had submitted over 40 million URLs to internet filters and identified 775,492 blocks, 21,776 of which are suspect false positives. This would suggest around 3 per cent of URLs are blocked incorrectly by these filters, which does illustrate why filtering cannot be as effective as some would like. The Open Rights Group, alongside Top10VPN, reported on this in 2019 (Top 10 VPN, 2019). The report states quite correctly that '[t]here is no evidence that filters are preventing children from seeing adult content or keeping them safe online. They may be contributing to a lack of resilience that can increase risk to children.'

In this section we delve further into the technology solutions available to homes and professionals in safeguarding and consider the impact of these when used as blunt tools. While we have only considered filtering until now, we will now explore two other classes of tool – monitoring and tracking. Monitoring, as with filtering, has its originals in school safeguarding, and was initially viewed as a more progressive approach to online safeguarding. While filtering blocked content, monitoring software would allow access to content, but raise alerts if that content was considered by the software logic to be harmful. When an alert was raised, a professional (in general a member of teaching staff) could judge whether the alert was valid and deal with the safeguarding incident if it was. However, the concept of monitoring has evolved a great deal, as we will explore later, and arguably now offers a more invasive and equally restrictive approach to safeguarding that has significant impact upon individuals' rights.

The central concept of any monitoring approach is simple – collect data on online access at a network or application level and develop response strategies accordingly. The basic techniques used to trigger alerts were initially similar to filtering – watch lists and keyword matching. An organisation can set parameters for the monitoring (for example, no pornography and gambling) and the software will make use of prescribed lists of websites identified in these categories and corpuses of keywords related to the two types of online activity. However, this is no longer the case and monitoring solutions are available in both home and educational settings that can, for example, capture message interaction and sharing, interception and 'interpret' image sharing and make attempts as assuming meaning of communications through artificial intelligence techniques such as Natural Language Processing.

However, even at a basic level, there are issues that arise. There is a notorious media story of a young man who triggered a terrorism alert as a result of trying to access the website for the UK Independence Party (as reported by the *Independent* newspaper, 2016). In 2015, as a result of concerns regarding the online radicalisation of young people by terrorist groups, the UK government (2015b) defined a number of duties of schools, referred to as part of the Prevent strategy, about tackling this issue. As a result of the combination of Prevent duties, and a monitoring system that raised an alert because the UK Independence Party's website was listed as a potentially harmful site (which, of itself, should raise concerns around freedom of expression of legitimate political parties), a young man was viewed as at potential risk of radicalisation and created significant media interest! The story illustrates two key issues:

- filtering software alerts are not necessarily very intelligent;
- without effective training, how might professionals be expected to respond?

As with filtering, schools have an expectation under the *Keeping Children Safe in Education* (DfE, 2018) statutory guidance to have 'appropriate' monitoring in place. And as with filtering, the guidance on what 'appropriate' is is defined outside of the statutory instrument. Within the school setting, the basic URL/keyword monitoring has now been superseded with other more active/proactive platforms that can work at a far more sophisticated level, for example being able to proactively monitor while a student is typing and making judgements on their intention as a result of this. The UK Safer Internet Centre (online) guidance on appropriate monitoring makes specific mention of the need for trained, knowable staff to respond to monitoring software alerts:

> Monitoring systems require capable and competent staff with sufficient capacity to effectively manage them, together with the support and

knowledge of the entire staff. Monitoring systems are there to safeguard children and the responsibility therefore should lie with the school leadership/governors and Designated Safeguarding Lead. Schools and Colleges should ensure that their staff and in particular those responsible for and managing their monitoring strategy have sufficient capacity and capability.

There is clear guidance that, within a school setting, the technology will not be an automated solution but a tool to support staff in making safeguarding judgements. This is, arguably, the best role for technology – collect data and raise alerts, but leave decision making to other stakeholders.

However, as monitoring approaches developed there has been significant evidence of feature creep in monitoring systems. While they used to function mainly around list-based interception and alerts, the technical capabilities of software and network systems means that the feature suite can now be far more complex. However, a fundamental question that rarely seems to be asked is because something is possible in a software system, should it be part of that system? Furthermore, there seems to be even less consideration of the rights of the individual(s) upon which these systems are imposed. Particularly if we are considering vulnerable adults, a key question when considering applying any of these systems should be 'does this impact upon their rights, and can they consent?'.

We are minded of the example previously explored in this book regarding spot-checking mobile devices in a residential sessing. Clearly there was intent there to ensure residents were safe from harm as a result of these checks. And there was obviously some consideration of consent because we were told that residents had consented. However, we would raise questions from both the safeguarding perspective (will this really ensure harm reduction?) and consent. Were the residents in a position to be able to consent? And what would have happened to them if they had not granted consent? Furthermore, while we frequently hear the statement 'safeguarding trumps data protection rights', this is not as clear cut as it seems. While there is provision in Schedule 8 of the Data Protection Act (UK Government, 2018) for processing of data without the consent of an individual, there are very specific conditions associated with this processing:

(3) For the purposes of this paragraph, an individual aged 18 or over is 'at risk' if the controller has reasonable cause to suspect that the individual—

(a) has needs for care and support,
(b) is experiencing, or at risk of, neglect or physical, mental or emotional harm, and

(c) as a result of those needs is unable to protect himself or herself against the neglect or harm or the risk of it.

These needs or harms would need to be clearly demonstrated to merit data processing for a safeguarding reason – we are concerned with no evidence to support this and decision to carry out data processing without the consent of the owner would not be supported by the legislation. Features in modern monitoring systems can be as wide-ranging as keystroke analysis (and keyword monitoring), live screen viewing, application monitoring and interception, real-time audio monitoring (listening in on a particular device in a classroom) and evidence capture features, which will collect data from the device (for example image capture from the device's camera, screen grabs and browsing history collection as a result of an alert). And there is historical evidence of incidents where monitoring software exceeds what is morally or legally acceptable.

Perhaps the most famous case of this was in schools in the US, brought to light in the case *Robbins v Lower Merion School District* (PacerMonitor, online). This case has been subject to much discussion and it is worthwhile exploring the salient points to highlight the issue of technology extending moral boundaries. While this took place against a backdrop of child safeguarding between a school and minors under their care, the scenario could be equally applicable to a vulnerable adult and their care team. In this case a number of schools in the Lower Merion School District in the US adopted a policy of providing students with laptops for use both in school and at home. The school district, quite rightly, raised concerns about laptops being provided by the schools (and therefore having a level of liability with the provider) and whether they might be used for non-school activities and inappropriate behaviour. They therefore decided to install monitoring software onto the laptops prior to distributing them to students. However, the software the schools decided to install far exceeded the safeguarding concern and equally demonstrated a covert attitude to the deployment of this monitoring software.

As a result, one of the schools involved in the scheme subjected a student to disciplinary procedures for what they referred to as inappropriate behaviour at home. When the student challenged this and questioned the evidence the school held to justify the disciplinary action, it was discovered that the laptops were not only monitoring internet access and application usage, but also sending a stream of images back to the school servers for analysis by staff. As a result of suspicions raised by Blake Robbins, the student being disciplined, it was ultimately discovered that over 66,000 images of students at his school were collected via these laptops using the built-in webcams on the laptops. As well as communicating images directly when an online connection was available, the monitoring software was also capable of collecting images locally and uploading them at a later time. While the school argued they had valid safeguarding reasons for collecting this data, it was clear from the case that consent had not been obtained, purpose for data collection specified, or expectations of data usage set. Even if there was a safeguarding concern, the fact that the image data was subsequently used in a student disciplinary action, something that moves the use of the data away from safeguarding concern to one of control clearly demonstrated this remit had far been exceeded without any consideration of the students' privacy or data protection rights. Even in the unlikely event of students consenting to image capture at home for safeguarding purposes, the use of this data for disciplinary purposes would far exceed this remit.

Furthermore, it was argued that given the schools took a proactive decision not to inform either students or parents of the installed monitoring software or request consent, there is evidence that the intention was covert, students' privacy had further been breached and the data had been collected for use in a control, rather than safeguarding, scenario. Unsurprisingly, the court found against the school district, and it was subject to a heavy fine. This case strongly highlights both the potential for abuse in a monitoring context with technology, and also the temptation to use this technology beyond its intention. It would be doubtful that, for example, the software platform used would have been advertised as 'collect[ing] images of children in their home and use this data to discipline them in school'. However, given that functionality exists there is a temptation to make use of the data available, regardless of data protection or sharing policies.

We need to bear in mind that algorithms are not very good with the interpretation of context. Therefore, consider the scenario where an adult with learning difficulties, P, is subject to monitoring software as their care team or residential setting has concerns they are accessing sexual content they consider to be inappropriate. Leaving aside the fact that we would doubt the legality of this assumption as a safeguarding concern, let us consider the impact of excessive monitoring in the situation. P decides to search for something on an LGBTQ site related to gender and sexuality, as is their right. We have seen from the Blocked project that many of these sites will be blocked, and we would expect some monitoring software to create alerts based upon these sites (particularly if using keyword-based strategies for identifying inappropriate content). If an alert is triggered, one would expect some sort of incident management process to commence. But how would the professionals respond in this scenario? One would hope that they would ignore the alert as it is clearly a false positive. However, they might decide that they might bring their own biases to the response and decide that if they are accessing this information it needs to be talked about with them. They might bring in other family members to discuss what P was searching and whether they had done anything like this before. What is clear is that, given there should be no safeguarding concerns in relation to accessing this sort of content, any such discussions would be a breach of P's privacy and their rights to access information. While we would hope that each alert is dealt with in a pragmatic and person-centric manner, we can see from the Lower Merion case or the story of the young man accessing the UK Independence Party website that this is not always the reality of the situation.

We should also note that two of the cases we explored in the previous chapter ([2020] EWCOP 24 and [2020] EWCOP 66) have examples of excessive screen time being used to demonstrate that an individual might not have capacity to engage with the internet and social media. Another clear example of the social construction of risk, screen time is another of those common risks associated with online harms, where many people seem to have an opinion that it must be harmful. "Surely," we have been asked, "if they're up to all hours online, it's going to have a negative impact on their well-being?" Sadly, as with most aspects of online safeguarding, it is not as straightforward as this. A lot of the policy discussion around screentime relates to children, but as we can see from Court of Protection proceedings, the notion of screentime can manifest itself in relation to vulnerable adults also.

In an interview in the *Times* of 10 March 2018 (The Times, 2018), the then Secretary of State for Digital, Culture, Media and Sport, Matt Hancock, announced plans to bring in legislation that would restrict the amount of time children and young people could use social media platforms online in a simple soundbite: 'There is genuine concern about the amount of screen time young people are clocking up and the negative impact it might have on their lives. It is right that we think about what more we could do in this area.' Mr Hancock went on to state that, in an unsurprising sense of déjà vu reagarding politicians voicing concerns around online harms, '[w]e are not afraid to legislate because it is our job to make sure laws are up to date'. Yet the evidence base around the relationship between screentime and its impact upon their well-being, is very immature and poorly understood. For a long time the American Association of Paediatrics (AAP) 2+2 guidance was viewed as a viable measure for screen time (Graber, 2015). This simply stated, with no empirical evidence, that children under two should not be online at all, and those between the ages of two and 16 should have a maximum of two hours screen time. Arbitrary blanket measures fail to acknowledge the different types of screen time that can occur – for example, was this someone passively consuming content or enjoying rich interaction with a multi-player gaming environment or educational content? While in recent times the AAP have revised this view to something more complex (American Academy of Paediatrics, 2016), the 2+2 rule is still often quoted.

A large study by Przbylski and Weinstein (2017) of the Oxford Internet Institute examined the data of 120,000+ UK teenagers and found that for 15-year-olds the effect of screen time on mental well-being depended on the category of screen time and was different for weekdays and weekends. It also noted that clear negative associations with screen time were far smaller than, for example, positive associations between well-being and eating breakfast regularly. Additionally, a more recent large-scale study by Orben and Przybylski (2019) argued that their data (which was multinational and detailed) showed little evidence of a link between screen time and well-being.

Nevertheless, this is another aspect of monitoring interest and leading to professional and familial arguments around how long someone should be allowed to be online. While we are certainly not advocating the unfettered, unmonitored access to whatever an individual wishes to see should be the default position, 'they are online too much' is not a reasoned, well-measured, safeguarding judgement.

However, screentime monitoring and image capture are not the only things that monitoring software can do. We are starting to see a class of what is reassuringly referred to as SafetyTech, that proposes the parent or carer can 'see everything, always' (this was an advertising strapline for one such provider). While we can see the financial incentive for selling concerned individuals certain products that will reassure them that the vulnerable are safe, will a software solution that feeds the controller a stream of websites access, messages sent, images exchanges and screentime used, actually do anything to safeguard the individual? And, we ask, is the massive breach of privacy justified?

We have had these discussions with both professionals and parents over the years. In these sessions there is usually a mix of those who think digital monitoring is a good and necessary thing and others who do not. A scenario we often present is: "If you have someone in your care of whom you are concerned, why not put a digital camera on them every morning so you can live stream their day to a monitoring device? You can watch their whole day and reassure yourself they are safe." Generally, this is viewed as a step too far by most in the training room. "Why?" we ask? "Because," they reply, "surely the invasion of privacy is justified if you can reassure yourself the individual is safe from harm?" At this point someone generally raises the fact that you are not ensuring they are safe from harm, you are just observing the harm that is occurring. And this is also true of monitoring systems that feed those with the power to access them with an endless stream of browsing history and communications. It would seem that we are confusing safety with surveillance, and because technology provides the methods to achieve this, we collect tool after tool that allows us to collect more and more data – convinced by the notion that they are, in some way, safe if we have all of this data.

The concept of safety is interesting in this context; the justification for the use of increasingly oppressive monitoring is that it is needed to *assure* safety. As we have discussed elsewhere in this book, guaranteeing safety online is not reasonable. We cannot prevent the risk of harm occurring, given the diversity of online activities. We can, however, help mitigate risk. We are, however, unconvinced that these software solutions help with this. While we can see positive uses of monitoring to ensure vulnerable people are not visiting websites with potentially harmful or illegal content, it gets to a point where the role become less one of carer, and more one of controller. There are indeed some risks that can be mitigated using this level of surveillance – for example the issues around grooming and contact from potential abusers might be mitigated by having access to contact lists and messaging. Yet these apps will only provide access to certain messaging platforms. While access to the mobile device's own telephony (that is, calls and SMS) is relatively straightforward, to access app-specific messaging is more problematic, which is generally why only major platforms (for example Facebook, Instagram, Snapchat, WhatsApp) are covered.

Monitoring therefore raises many interesting tensions between safeguarding and rights. Regardless of the approach, there are some very real impacts on privacy, in particular, as a result of these tools, but also on rights such as freedom of expression and access to the media and, in the case of *covert* monitoring, placing significant restriction on respecting the views of the individual being monitored.

By way of illustration, a recent BBC News (2019c) report had a parent justifying their own approach to the question they had posed of 'so how can we keep them safe from harmful content?' It seems, in the case of this article (and this resonates with our own conversations with some parents), it is to look at everything they do online:

> My two daughters, aged 11 and 13, loudly protest about 'violations of privacy' when they realised I could see every site and app they've visited.
>
> Once I've reassured them that this is not about snooping, but more about limitation and safety, they grudgingly seem to accept the new controls.

French philosopher Michel Foucault's (1975) work on discipline and punishment has frequently been drawn upon when considering the role of surveillance technologies in modern society (Boyle, 2017). In particular, Foucault's interpretation of Bentham's physical Pantopicon – the architectural physical structure, see in some prison buildings around the world, where the inmate can see nothing but the means of their own surveillance, whereas the controlling sentinel can observe everything the inmate does (Leaton Gray and Phippen, 2017).

Foucault observes that in such a system, the subject of the surveillance becomes the object of information, never a subject in communication. If the child or vulnerable adult is the object of information, and has such stringent monitoring and surveillance technologies imposed on them, using the excuse that 'we need to see everything you do to ensure that you are safe' (as noted earlier, the advertising strapline of one of these providers is the somewhat chilling 'See everything. Always'), we are potentially imposing an unacceptable level of control and data collection upon them because what we are actually wishing to achieve is not a safe individual, but a compliant one. Let us once again return to the mobile phone spot checks. Are these being do to check safety or to give the individual the message 'if you do anything we disagree with on that phone, we'll know about it'? Or, to rephrase it 'remember we're watching you', somewhat reminiscent the Orwellian nightmarish 1984.

The individual is observed, with no power to prevent this, and plays no part in the surveillance scenario, other than providing the observer with information about their behaviour. The panopticon asserts the *automatic functioning of power*, where the subject knows they are being watched, but can do nothing about it. In a scenario where a carer can see everything related to an individual's online life always, we are experiencing the application of a digital panopticon where the individual is the object of information and the carer is the observer and controller. With the application of technology that proposes that a carer can see every communication, image or keystroke on a device, while they might justify this surveillance as a means to reassure themselves that this is the only way the individual will be kept safe, we are establishing power imbalance that has long been viewed as a model of control.

This is perhaps highlighted most keenly with the growing use of Global Position System (GPS) tracking technology implemented in either dedicated physical devices (such as trackable wristbands) or as a function of a mobile device. GPS tracking is becoming increasingly mainstream; we speak to children whose parents track them, we speak to carers who track individuals in their care and we speak to couples who track each other 'because we love each other'. While techniques might differ, the premise is the same: an app is installed, or a tracking function is on a device, and this allows the controller to see where the observed individual is. Software can also be used to set alerts should the observed move away from a prescribed location, much as one might do tracking a tagged criminal. We must, once again, reflect upon whether the safeguarding justification for the use of such technology is borne out in the actual application. We have, on one occasion, heard of a positive use of this technology – a young adult with severe epilepsy was somewhat restricted to the home because of the risk of his having a fit while outside, and his family were concerned in this event they would be unable to find him. In this case, with his full agreement, the family made use of mobile phone tracking so he had an opportunity to be out more, with the reassurance that if he did have a seizure he could be found. This case is a good illustration of the fact that the application of SafetyTech should be considered on a case-by-case basis. However, in most cases it is rarely justified and in the best interests of the individual.

It is interesting to note that recent guidance from the UK Sentencing Council (2018) has begun to explicitly refer to GPS tracking as evidence of coercion and control in relationships, and in a domestic abuse case it might be used as a justification for a harsher sentence. However, this technology is also applied far too easily in the safeguarding scenarios as a measure with sinister undertones – expanding from 'if you do anything on your phone we don't like, we'll know about it', the control can be extended to 'we will always know where you are'. Again, this is another technology where the façade of safeguarding can be used to exert more control rather than empowerment.

Foucault (1975) defined the concept of the *Docile Body* as 'one that may be subjected, used, transformed, and improved. And that this docile body can only be achieved through strict regimen of disciplinary acts'; in essence, a malleable object on which disciplinary force is acted in order that it might be controlled, and therefore more useful to those who hold power. After all, a docile body is less likely to challenge authority or disobey. He referred to the role of observation and surveillance in the achievement of the docile body within 18th-century military structures: 'In the perfect military camp, all power would be exercised solely through exact observation; each gaze would form a part of the overall functioning of power.' He also explored the role of technology in achieving this:

[S]ide by side with the major technology of the telescope, the lens and the light beam, which were an integral part of the new physics and cosmology, there were the minor techniques of multiple and intersecting observations, of eyes that must see without being seen; using techniques if subjugation and methods of exploitation, an obscure art of light and the visible was secretly preparing a new knowledge of man.

It is interesting to reflect upon what Foucault might have made of the modern technologies used to control. Clearly tracking is rarely used to keep an individual safe – they are made aware that technologies are used to know where they are and whether they were being compliant (or perhaps docile?). In the late 1970s the psychologist Jack Flasher (1978) coined the term *Adultism* to refer to the prejudice adults can exert on children from a position of privilege and judgement, to challenge their worldview because it is different to their own while having the requisite power (financial, legislative, physical, and so on) to restrict young people's lives. We see adultist elements in the broad online safeguarding policy space and also the responses of other stakeholders to keeping the vulnerable safe.

The cybersecurity expert Bruce Schneier, in 2006, observed the impact of surveillance on the population as a whole:

For if we are observed in all matters, we are constantly under threat of correction, judgment, criticism, even plagiarism of our own uniqueness. We become children, fettered under watchful eyes, constantly fearful that – either now or in the uncertain future – patterns we leave behind will be brought back to implicate us, by whatever authority has now become focused upon our once-private and innocent acts. We lose our individuality, because everything we do is observable and recordable.

There is, however, a fundamental flaw in this digital panopticon. Unlike the physical panopticon, where the structures of the environment mean the observed is powerless, this is not the case in the online world. Those who wish to control need to bear in mind that the digital panopticon is easier to break out of than the physical one. We have had many conversations with young people about whether they knew how to circumvent monitoring technology. They will find ways to do this, be it using a different device, making use of proxying or encryption, or even something as simple as switching the device off (in the case of being aware they are being tracked). While the information, and power imbalance, is afforded to the controller by the tools at their disposal, the knowledge gap that often exists between the monitor and the monitored means that they can often bypass the constraints imposed upon them while still projecting a façade of passivity.

The need for a more critical response

We risk, as a community, a dystopian vision of safeguarding, where control is viewed as preferable to empowerment and human rights, with a view that technology can help us meet our needs to control behaviour and therefore mitigate risk. While, in our exploration of the law and Court of Protection proceedings, we see increasingly progressive thinking around the individual, and the need for sharp, focused intervention rather than blunt tools, we have seen in this chapter that a lack of knowledge results, even with the best of intentions, from interventions that are controlling and invasive, and certainly not in the best interests of the individual.

The debates on care versus control and protection versus participation are further explored in the next chapter, which departs a little from the trajectory of the book to this point in that it examines vulnerability in relation to mental health as an aspect of mental capacity and associated online harms from content – namely that of pro-harm content. And in the chapter following on from that that we will consider, instead, what a more progressive, rights-based approach might look like, and how professionals can best support those they are working with.

6

Pro-harm content online

Introduction

As we explore in Chapter 2, one of the key areas of online risk relates to *content risk* and it is the concerns related to harmful content that this chapter explores in detail. It takes as its focus the recent media and public discourse on the risk of content associated with mental health issues – namely pro-harm content, for example self-harm, suicide and eating disorders. 'The internet is arguably now the major source of mental health information available to the public' (Jorm, 2019b: 364). There is increasing concern about the widespread impact of online harms on mental health and while much of the focus of the chapters in this book centres around mental capacity, for example relating to a learning disability or following a brain injury, this chapter more specifically focuses on the debate on mental health and online content. It explores the research and the available evidence in relation to what is known as pro-harm content online relating to three key areas of concern – non-suicidal self-harm (NSSH), suicidal ideation and eating disorders. Research to date suggests that there is a complex relationship between mental capacity and mental health and the increasing use of what are often referred to as 'pro-sites' by vulnerable adults. However, as we have argued elsewhere, vulnerability is not a static concept (Phippen and Bond, 2021). While there may not be previously acknowledged mental capacity issues, mental health may have a significant impact on mental capacity. According to the RHC report (Sharrat, 2020) on online harm, reporting of harmful content, including graphic/violent content, self-harm/suicide content or violent pornography and sexualised self-harm, is on the increase. Using examples from what Oksanen et al (2016) term *harm-advocating online content* in relation to pro-eating disorders, pro-self-harm and pro-suicide online communities and forums, this chapter examines the phenomenon of harm-advocating online content, its significance in understanding and managing mental health, and the importance of understanding its influence on mental health. It is important to understand how and why people use harm-advocating online content to learn about and seek acceptance and belonging in an online community and how this behaviour may prevent recovery. It has been well recognised that the vulnerable use such sites as they often experience a lack of acceptance and understanding in the 'real world' and find a sense of belonging and friendship online with like-minded others.

It has long been acknowledged that social media enable communication, collaboration and community building yet simultaneously open up new possibilities for criminal behaviours and for victimisation (Yar, 2006), and the internet has provided a space for marginalised and stigmatised groups to meet, share and exchange information. 'Key to the political appeal of the internet is its potentially disruptive implications for the public/private divide, including its capacity to enable "privatised" voices to become public' (Slater, 2017: 39). As the Royal College of Psychiatry (2020: 65) states:

> Digital technology is now a central part of peoples' lives, for information, entertainment and communication, particularly social media platforms such as Facebook, Tumblr and Twitter. The use of apps accessed on mobile devices is now a way of life, so people can share, connect and communicate with each other instantly and spontaneously. People use a range of social media platforms and congregate within online forums, which have quickly been gaining popularity due to the easy sharing and anonymity they offer.
>
> While anonymity features can be associated with bullying, these sites also allow people to share and explore difficult issues they are experiencing in their lives, such as anxiety, self-image concerns, and relationships, away from the eyes of others. They may also share thoughts and feelings concerning self-harm and suicide, which may be accompanied by images, videos, or blogs etc.

Websites and discussion forums have become an important and sometimes controversial source of information on suicide (Westerlund et al, 2016), NSSH and eating disorders (Bond, 2012; 2018). The debate on the online phenomenon of pro-harm content on websites, blogs and social media platforms emerged well over a decade ago and has been the subject of differing legal responses globally, and concerns over people's relationship with social media and their mental health are increasingly appearing in both academic discourse and media headlines. As we observe in Chapter 2, much of the public and political anxiety relating to pro-harm content has concentrated on protectionist discourses around children and young people. For example, the UKCCIS (2016: 7) publication includes 'promoting harmful behaviour such as self-harm, suicide, pro-anorexia, bulimia' as a risk to children, however, as Lyle et al (2016: 117) point out, there is 'no specific definition of illegal content'. These concerns are set out in the joint ministerial foreword in the *Online Harms* White Paper (UK Government, 2019), which states:

> Other online behaviours or content, even if they may not be illegal in all circumstances, can also cause serious harm. The internet can

be used to harass, bully or intimidate, especially people in vulnerable groups or in public life. Young adults or children may be exposed to harmful content that relates, for example, to self-harm or suicide. These experiences can have serious psychological and emotional impact.

Mental health and the internet

Both public and media discourses on mental health and social media in relation to pro-harm content centre on concerns based on both *normalisation* and *contagion* and that mental health problems, for example anorexia, are glamorised. In recent years many parents, advocates and policy makers have expressed concerns regarding the potential negative impact of social media use (Berryman et al, 2018) on young people's mental health. In the UK, for example, the tragic case of teenager Molly Russell's suicide attracted considerable media attention, 'not least because her father has pressed forcibly the case for the damaging effect of social media and the need to suppress content that might (in his view, definitely does) encourage suicide' (House, 2020: 132). The media focus on internet-related behaviour is not, however, limited to children and young people, as illustrated by the newspaper reports of Rose Patterson's suicide aged 63 in June 2020, which detailed the use of the internet in taking her own life (see, for example, Bhatia and Tingle writing in the *Daily Mail* on 22 September 2020). Furthermore, the Coroner in the Patterson case, John Ellery, was reported in the *Guardian* as saying: 'Ms Paterson's intentions could be established from the fact she was found in a remote area, and internet searches made between 27 May and 23 June' (Morris, 2020).

However, both these examples of media accounts, and other examples like them which imply that online content is a causal factor in mental health, reflect technological deterministic approaches and fail to acknowledge that both risk and risk anxiety are complex social and cultural constructions. As we argue throughout this book, our everyday lives, our identities, communities and relationships are interwoven with people and technologies, with offline and online, and, as such, we need a better understanding of the dynamic and multifarious nature of vulnerability online (Phippen and Bond, 2021). Furthermore, online content is not simply passively consumed by users, but also produced and shared by users in a complicated interplay of online interactions. It is therefore important to remember that 'digital culture is described as participatory culture where users do not only consume information but also contribute to it in a variety of ways' (Uzelac, 2008: 17). As such, 'social media provides its participants with more than an open platform for testimony; it is also a space of entertainment, creativity and social interaction' (Vitis and Gilmor, 2016: 6), and the mobilisation of everyday technologies has transformed people's access to social media (Bond, 2014).

This is important to understanding not only how people, including those with a learning disability, interact and experience online environments, but also pro-harm cultures online and the multifaceted relationship between mental health and social media. Furthermore, it should be remembered that mental health has different meanings in different contexts. Pilgrim (2020: 3) defines mental health as follows: 'Mental health is used positively to indicate a state of psychological wellbeing, negatively to indicate its opposite (as in "mental health problems") or euphemistically to indicate facilities used by, or imposed upon, people with mental health problems (as in "mental health services").'

According to McManus et al (2019b), mental health is one of the most pervasive contextual factors for suicidal thoughts, suicide attempt and NSSH. They concluded from their study that this held true for the population as a whole and for specific subgroups with both depression and anxiety disorders, each having an independent association. The more severe the symptoms of mental illness, the stronger the association was with suicidal thoughts and self-harm behaviour. The relationship between mental health and social media has been the focus of a growing body of research both in the UK and across the globe. Risk is both increased and ameliorated through interactions online as research to date suggests that there are both negative and positive effects of social media in relation to mental health. While, some studies have indicated that social media use may be tied to negative mental health outcomes, including suicidality, loneliness and decreased empathy, other studies have not found evidence for harm or have indicated that social media use may be beneficial for some individuals (Berryman et al, 2018). Additionally, it is interesting to note from Coyne et al's (2020) recently published longitudinal study that time spent using social media was not related to individual changes in depression or anxiety over eight years.

In May 2020 RHC, the UK's national reporting centre for harmful online content, found a correlation between poor mental health and viewing harmful online content, including graphic/violent content, self-harm/suicide content and pornography. Thirty-two per cent of RHC clients described viewing such content, often inadvertently, as having a negative impact on their mental health with 13 per cent reporting suicidal ideation (Sharrat, 2020). It is also noteworthy that people who are depressed are more likely to go online to communicate (Hwang et al, 2009) and that mental health is a common topic on pro-harm communities and forums. Oksanen et al's (2016) study found that a lower level of happiness and previous online and offline victimisation experiences were associated with exposure to harm-advocating online material but there were gender differences in the type of harm-advocating online content used, with females more likely to view eating-disorder online content but males more likely to view pro-self-harm and pro-suicide content online.

Pro-non-suicidal self-harm and suicide

The history of suicide shows that it has been documented since ancient times (Kapur and Goldney, 2019) and became the focus of sociological study with the publication of Durkeim's (1897/1951) monograph. According to the ONS (2020), there were 5,691 suicides registered in England and Wales in 2019, with an age-standardised rate of 11.0 deaths per 100,000 population and consistent with the rate in 2018. Around three-quarters of registered deaths in 2019 were among men (4,303 deaths), which follows a consistent trend back to the mid 1990s. However according to the ONS (2020), despite having a low number of deaths overall, rates among the under 25s have generally increased in recent years, particularly in 10 to 24-year-old females, where the rate has increased significantly since 2012 to its highest level with 3.1 deaths per 100,000 females in 2019. However, the causes of suicide are complex (Kapur and Goldney, 2019); as the Royal College Psychiatrists (2020: 69) observe, 'suicide is a complex behaviour with multiple aetiological factors, some of which are poorly understood'. This is very important but seemingly overlooked or unhelpfully ignored in the cases outlined earlier which apportion blame to internet use. According to Mind, a national UK charity providing information and support for mental health, anyone can have suicidal feelings, whatever their background or situation in life, and such feelings can be a symptom of an existing mental health problem or episode of mental distress, or sometimes a side-effect of a psychiatric or other medication. Furthermore, some people experience suicidal feelings because of traumatic life events.

The Samaritans, the leading UK-based charity for suicide prevention, outline the risks associated with self-harm and suicide content online, which include the promotion, encouragement and glorification of self-harm and suicide, the sharing of information about methods of harm, social contagion and imitative or 'copycat suicides' (Samaritans, 2020). McTernan and Ryan (2020: 8) further argue that 'there is significant risk of harm related to online behaviour such as reinforcement, stigmatization, normalisation, triggering and contagion, in addition to hindering professional help-seeking and the depiction of methods of suicidal behaviour'. A clear example of this is can be found in the case study of a Swedish online suicide forum published in the *British Journal of Psychiatry* by Westerlund et al (2016) that found that nearly half the posted messages before the act of suicide encouraged the victim to complete the suicidal act, and a surprising number of posts after the suicide act expressed excitement, although around half of the posts did consider the successful suicide to be 'tragic'.

In the UK the Royal College of Psychiatrists (2020) consider self-harm to be one of the strongest predictors of suicide, including among older people. The Mental Health Foundation (2021) define self-harm as follows:

Self-harm is when someone intentionally hurts or injures themselves. For some, self-harm can represent a way of coping with or expressing feelings and emotions that are overwhelming or overpowering. Self-harm can refer to any behaviour where someone intentionally causes harm to themselves. It can be any behaviour, minor or high-risk, which causes injury or harm.

As self-harm can refer to a range of behaviours, estimates of how common it actually is can vary between studies. McManus et al (2019a) looked at trends over time and analysed the data from three years' Adult Psychiatric Morbidity surveys in the UK (2000, 2007 and 2014) and found that the prevalence of self-reported lifetime NSSH increased from 2·4 per cent (2·0–2·8) in 2000, to 6·4 per cent (5·8–7·2) in 2014. Increases in prevalence were noted in both sexes and across age groups – most notably in women and girls aged 16–24 years, in whom prevalence increased from 6·5 per cent (4·2–10·0) in 2000, to 19·7 per cent (15·7–24·5) in 2014. Yet, as the authors of the study point out, most people who self-harm do not present to hospitals, so whether this rise reflects an increase in the prevalence of self-harm in the community is unknown.

As suggested earlier in this chapter, concerns have been raised about people accessing pro-self-harm content online and there is evidence from some studies to suggest that engaging with harm-advocating content online normalises the condition. Other studies, however, have found positive benefits for users in these communities in the form of social support, acceptance and understanding. From their systematic review of 46 independent studies of internet use, self-harm and suicidal behaviour in young people, Marchant et al (2017: 2), for example, concluded that 'there is significant potential for harm from online behaviour (normalisation, triggering, com- petition, contagion) but also the potential to exploit its benefits (crisis support, reduction of social isolation, delivery of therapy, outreach)'. Similarly, Dyson et al's (2016) systematic review of social media use to discuss and view deliberate self-harm acts concluded that many studies identify both beneficial and detrimental effects on users. This dualism is important. Lavis and Winter's (2020) study of peer support around self-harm on social media, which reviewed Twitter, Reddit and Instagram, found that peer support is the central focus of online interactions around self-harm and that those accessing self-harm content are likely to already be self-harming. Similar to Bond's (2012 and 2018) work on pro-eating disorder communities, which is discussed later, Lavis and Winter (2020: 842) found that users turn to social media to 'understand, and seek help for, their actions and feelings in a context of offline stigma and service support gaps'. Understanding this motivation to seek help and support is essential in effectively responding to harm-advocating content and pro-harm communities. It is therefore interesting to note that one study of images tagged as self-harm on social media published in the *British Media Journal* goes so far as to argue:

> Findings suggest that clinicians should not be overly anxious about what is being posted on social media. Although we found a very few posts suggesting self-injury was attractive, there were no posts that could be viewed as actively encouraging others to self-harm. Rather, the sites were being used to express difficult emotions in a variety of creative ways, offering inspiration to others through the form of texts or shared messages about recovery. (Shanahan et al, 2019: 1)

Pro-eating disorders

Mental health conditions often overlap and are interrelated. Thus, talk of mental health, self-harm and suicide is common on pro-eating disorder communities online. Such posts are mainly responded to with responses from others sending messages of friendship and support and advice about coping with suicidal thoughts (Bond, 2012; 2018). The communities also share ideas with each other on health-related problems like hair loss, general advice on living with an eating disorder as well as extreme dietary advice on how to lose more weight and how to hide their condition from family, friends and medical practitioners and thus become a *better anorexic*. Like self-harm, it is through both medicalisation and stigmatisation that participants of the pro-eating disorder communities become marginalised and seek others who share their beliefs to find effective support and through actively visiting and maintaining pro-eating disorder (pro-ana) websites, weblogs and personal pages (Haas et al, 2011).

It is such concerns related to both the content and the potentially dangerous advice on extreme weight loss that underpin the debates on the legality/illegality of the sites and calls for harm-advocating content to be banned. However, it has been argued for some time that 'the focus on websites as the cause of eating disorders and poor body image is misplaced' (Gailey, 2009: 93). Certainly, in wider society, especially in mainstream fashion media, the promotion of the ultra-thin body remains uncontested, and in fact celebrated, yet condemned by the media and by policy makers as disordered, harmful and dangerous when viewed in pro-eating disorder online communities (Bond, 2012; 2018). As 'western bodies tend to prioritise the visual sense' (Mellor and Shilling, 1997: 6), it is essential that this debate on online risk begins to critically consider the normalisation of the thin body in mainstream culture and fashion media more generally and the way that cultural settings influence the perceptions of and people's experiences of a stigmatised mental illness, including the way they communicate and express themselves online and offline.

It is important to remember that people with an eating disorder are also likely to suffer from other mental health issues and frequently suffer from depression or social anxiety (Jurarascio et al, 2010). The need to be thin stems in part from having low self-esteem (Karpowicz et al, 2009) and these sites allow stigmatised or socially isolated individuals to share experiences anonymously in a 'rich tapestry of identity work' (Giles, 2006). The representations of the ultra-thin body – the images – and the descriptions of those lived experiences in the pursuit of the ultra-thin body – the textual information – are both viewed as harmful to those who engage online viewing the ultra-thin body and consuming the pro-ana content. It is through these complex interactions that the ultra-thin body – the anorexic body – becomes normalised, and it is the normalising tendencies of extreme behaviours and images that constitute a social harm as being underweight is a signal of success (Borzekowski et al, 2010).

Just as with other issues associated with self-harm, people with eating disorders often lack social support (Tiller et al, 1997) and this need for social support, combined with technological developments which allow new online communities to develop quickly with no financial cost, has led to the plethora of pro-eating disorder websites, online forums and communities now online (Bond, 2012). It is both the secretive nature of pro-ana and the intimacy that people feel towards the disease itself and one another that make online environments ripe for self-disclosure (Hass et al, 2011). As such, concealing anorexic practice is part over everday life therefore, yet is reversed as a symbolic state as users struggle not only to reassert their self-determination, but also to attempt to regain their identity, albeit an anorexic identity (Rich, 2006).

The pro-ana community is substantial (Harshbarger, 2009) and the popularity of social networking sites which have captured common communication and self-identity discourse is reflected in the number of pro-ana groups on such sites, which are more focused on social aspects like interaction and social support (Jurarascio et al, 2010). Users of pro-ana websites score higher on a desire for thinness, perfectionism and Body Mass Index (BMI) and in positive attitudes towards pro-ana websites (Custers and Van den Bulck, 2009).

The relationship between an eating disorder and lifestyle choice is explored in much of the published literature on the subject and it is perhaps helpful to consider that 'lifestyle' does not necessarily imply a notion of choice; 'rather, it is a lifestyle in the sense of a "way of life" that pervades every aspect of the person's thought, perception and action' (Csipke and Horne, 2007). Current concerns in relation to viewing pro-ana images are therefore not just in relation to those with an eating disorder as there is strong evidence that exposure to pro-ana websites has immediate and negative effects on young women. 'Regarding behavioural expectations, pro-anorexia website viewers [women without a history of an eating disorder] reported that viewing the website made them more likely to exercise and think about their weight in the near future (today or tomorrow) than if they had not seen the website' (Bardone-Cone and Cass, 2006: 544). Even modest exposure to pro- eating disorder websites can encourage significant changes in calorie consumption and increased disordered eating behaviours (Jett et al, 2010). Caution, however, needs to be exercised in that the pro-ana community should not be viewed as a universally coherent standpoint (Giles, 2006). This observation is supported by a study of content (pro-ana, anti-ana, and pro-recovery) by Branley and Covey (2017) which found that extreme pro-ana posts were in the minority compared to anti-ana and pro-recovery, with pro-ana posts (including 'thinspiration') being more common on Twitter than Tumblr, whereas anti-ana and pro-recovery posts were more common on Tumblr.

What do we know?

It is clear from the research to date that the relationship between mental health and social media is complex and in relation to the pro-harm content online debate there are both potentially negative but also potentially positive outcomes for users. From a safegarding perspective, it is vitally important that online interactions are not considered in isolation from other factors and wider environments. The internet is a major source of information about mental health but a number of studies suggest that the quality of the information available online is very varied (see, for example, Reavely and Jorm, 2011). Viewing social media as having a straightforward causal effect on mental health is unhelpful and blames the technology without giving due consideration to the other actants in the network. Technological determinism masks the wider complexity of social media use and mental health (Bond, 2012; 2018) and allows us to avoid examining the wider social and structural contexts that give rise to both self-harm and social media use, and to ignore the fact that social media is a mirror of society (Lavis and Winter, 2020: 851).

When considering safeguarding adults online, it is important to recognise the existence of harm-advocating and extreme online communities and the relative ease with which people may encounter this material and the communities producing it (Oksanen et al, 2016: 11). However, while the pro-harm phenomenon is highly visible, easily accessed on a wide range of social media and reportedly a concern for policy makers, the underlying factors that led to its existence in the first place and its continuing popularity remain invisible and ignored. If we view individuals in pro-harm communities as victims rather than as criminals, a different perspective emerges. It is quite apparent from the research to date that the voices of the users of pro-harm content are largely absent. Rather than demonising these communities, we need a better understanding of mental health, internet use and social media, especially in relation to pro-harm content and the lived realities of those people who engage with these vibrant and highly active global communities. Thus, we argue in conclusion that responding effectively and appropriately to the pro-harm phenomenon is more problematic than simply criminalising it as, because it is viewed as deviant, such responses fail to address the very reasons why people engage in these virtual spaces in the first place.

> Two levels of essential support were highlighted by the people we spoke with: to manage chronic, ongoing stress, and to address acute tipping points and crises. Many people had little idea what support was available, some had looked for support and couldn't find any. Calls for better signposting and clear sources of information are a familiar mantra, but the issues remain. (McManus et al, 2019b: 7)

Pro-harm content is gaining visibility online and increased media attention which influences public and political discourse to control it but policy responses focus on the content itself rather than on the behaviours on which the content is based (Boyd et al, 2011). We cannot continue to ignore the harm caused by poor mental health services and a lack of effective support for those with mental health problems, which is unhelpfully overlooked and downplayed in the pro-harm debate. As Lavis and Winter (2020: 282) argue,

> [i]t is crucial to understand this in a less siloed way, reflecting how a variety of hashtags are used as conduits into a space of listening to the distress than underpins diagnostic labels. It is this distress that we need to bear in mind when considering social media use, in policy, in practice and in society.

When it comes to understanding social media, internet content and mental health, especially in relation to pro-harm content, we argue that there are a number of approaches to helpfully further our understanding. Rather than adopting a technological deterministic approach (in that technology is seen as either the problem or conversely the solution), but instead viewing the social phenomenon through the lens of zemiology, it becomes more apparent that harm-advocating content and pro-harm communities online as a social harm did not appear in a vacuum divorced from wider society (Slater, 2017: 39). The concept of *stigma* in relation to mental health is also important in that 'the efforts of stigmatized persons not only "normify" their own conduct but also encourage others to embody the stigmatised behaviour' (Goffman, 1963: 108). Eating disorders revolve around privacy and secrets (Kirwood, 2005) as do self-harm and suicidal ideation. Social support is 'a crucial buffer against mental health problems' and chronic personal isolation increases 'the risk of both depression and psychosis' and 'both are reduced in probability in those people who are part of a supportive network' (Pilgrim, 2020: 61). The anonymity of pro-harm culture provides safe spaces where people can talk openly, share their experiences and display their true self as part of a supportive network. It is through the establishment of an audience that users co-construct personal identities that are in keeping with the group (Haas et al, 2011). Stigma, both societal and internalised, is a clear motivation, as are offline service gaps and long waiting lists, and there is a need for a 'franker consideration of how self-harm is responded to in service settings, as well as society more broadly' (Lavis and Winter, 2020: 849).

Conclusion

The UK government's *Online Harms* White Paper (2020) sets out the harmful content or activity in the scope of the White Paper in a table based on an assessment of their prevalence and impact on individuals and society. Yet, as we have already argued, the White Paper also fails to acknowledge the lack of robust empirical evidence relating to 'online harms' and therefore fails to adequately explain how they intend to prioritise regulatory action to address the harms that have the greatest impact (Phippen and Bond, 2019b). Furthermore, as House (2020: 132) points out, the White Paper 'bundled encouraging self-harm or suicide with incitement to terrorist activities, dissemination of child pornography, and drug dealing on the dark web. The main direction has not therefore been about self-harm and suicide prevention, but about steps to regulate the tech giants'. As such, we also suggest, 'when it comes to policy discussions, attention focuses on trying to regulate the content or the services that host the content. Not only are such approaches often legally and technically untenable, but they also naively presume that eliminating problematic content will reduce the underlying practices' (see Boyd et al, 2011: 3). Therefore, rather than focusing the debate on whether or not to criminalise the content, it may be more helpful to consider why people set pro-harm sites up and use them in the first place. As people are increasingly using social media to communicate distress, particularly to peers (Marchant et al, 2017: 2), Branley and Covey (2017) suggest that developers of future interventions targeting negative pro-harm content should remain aware of the need to avoid any detrimental impact on positive online support.

The legal debate on harm-advocating content online remains contested as pro-harm communities are seemingly well recognised as a social harm in public and political debate. However, while the focus remains on the online spaces as the problem, too little is being done to actually help and support those with mental health problems as there is a dearth of effective support services and the few that are available are hard to access. As House (2020: 131) argues, '[u]nfortunately, participation in the public debate about this dilemma has been restricted and high-profile discussion of necessary action has been focused almost entirely on how much suppression of content is justified' and professional bodies 'should be doing much more than they are to shape how the debate is conducted'.

In moving this debate forward, Marchant et al (2017: 2) contend that the focus should now be on how specific media (social media, video/image sharing) might be used in therapy and recovery and that clinicians working with 'people who self-harm or have mental health issues should engage in discussion about internet use. This should be a standard item during assessment.' The Royal College of Psychiatrists (2020: 63) agree, stating that it 'is critical for professionals to include a person's digital life within their clinical assessments, especially when there are concerns about mental health'. They suggest typical lines of enquiry about internet and social media usage could usefully include whether the person:

- uses social media to access support for self-harm – through peer support or online fora, or reading information;
- provides support to other people;
- publicly shares their self-harming behaviour online;
- has many followers on sites they use;
- has been invited by online means to do things they would rather not do;
- has been subjected to negative reactions, threats, bullying or harassment online.

It is of great importance to increase awareness of suicide signals and understanding about how to respond to individuals who communicate suicide intentions on different forums on the internet (Westerland et al, 2016: 476). Additionally, in responding more effectively to pro-harm content in safeguarding, Horne and Wiggins (2009: 182) helpfully suggest:

> [I]t would seem that our research can suggest some implications for therapists, helpline staff and medical professionals – the ways in which receipting and validating identities can be important. It is important to treat a person who constructs a suicidal identity as one with individual problems – and not to try and generalise or minimise, but reconstruct identities with alternative rationalities where possible. Trying to solve problems suggests there is an easy answer, which invalidates the identity of 'suicidal'. Most importantly, it would appear that validating identities, especially when coming from those who are in a similar position, can be of great support.

The *Online Harms* White Paper (2020) states that '[a]ll users, children and adults, should be empowered to understand and manage risks so that they can stay safe online'. However, while the paper states that the government has taken steps to address digital literacy in the school curriculum, the steps it intends to take to support digital literacy for adults are less clear. Given that the table of harms in the paper includes harms with would relate to particularly vulnerable groups, no mention is made of empowering more vulnerable users.

We explore in the next chapter how empowering and supporting more vulnerable users is key to online safeguarding and how the need to ensure that mental health professionals and others working with and supporting people who have mental health problems or mental capability limitations need themselves to be digitally literate. The NHS (online) *A Health and Care Digital Capability Framework* (NHS, n.d.) uses Health Education England's definition of digital literacy as 'the capabilities that fit someone for living, learning, working, participating and thriving in a digital society' and includes '[t]he ability to use digital technologies in ways that support personal wellbeing and safety and the wellbeing and safety of others' (NHS, n.d.: 27). When considering digital literacy in relation to pro-harm content though, the concept of mental health literacy is also key to supporting and developing critical digital literacy for understanding the use of these online spaces. Jorm (2012: 231) suggests mental health literacy includes:

- knowledge of how to prevent mental disorders;
- recognition of when a disorder is developing;
- knowledge of help-seeking options and treatments available;
- knowledge of effective self-help strategies for milder problems;
- first aid skills to support others who are developing a mental health disorder or are in mental health crisis.

A 'notable feature of how this concept has been defined is that it is not simply knowledge of mental disorders or mental health, but rather knowledge that a person can use to take practical action to benefit their own mental health and that of others' (Jorm, 2019a: 53).

Therefore, we argue that while previous calls to ban these sites and restrict access to such content have been ineffectual, effective strategies to support vulnerable adults online and develop their understanding of how and why they are using them are desperately needed. Such advice, alongside providing pro-recovery support in a non-judgemental way, can enable a more realistic understanding of their mental health, including developing their knowledge of the factors underlying why they are seeking support online. This can lead to users understanding that more effective support may also be sought elsewhere that offers more positive and health-promoting information and advice.

7

'What works' in safeguarding adults online? Understanding the actors and the networks

Introduction

This chapter explores best practice in policy and practice around online safeguarding for vulnerable adults and those with capacity issues. It argues that there is an urgent need for more nuanced, individualised and progressive approaches for responding to online safeguarding for vulnerable adults that focus on their best interests for an informed assessment of their needs that does not unnecessarily negatively impact on their liberty. The aim of this book is to critically engage with the challenges and the tensions that arise from protectionist and participation discourses to interrogate these polarised standpoints and provide a more detailed understanding of the complexity of vulnerable adults engaging in everyday online activities and relationships. We highlight throughout the flawed approach and limitations of current legislative approaches and the worrying lack of knowledge in the current workforce but end with some excellent guidance from a highly experienced professional, James Codling. At the time of writing, recent practice across many sectors working with those with capacity issues has resulted in too many individuals having their rights to freedom of expression, privacy and access to information withdrawn, based on safeguarding arguments adopted as an excuse to excessively monitor and control individuals, which undermines their human rights (including the UNCRPD).

As Moser (2000: 201) argues,

> [T]he normalisation approach is constantly counteracted by processes that systematically produce inequality and reproduce exclusions: the main problem is a norm which locates agency, mobility and a centred subjectivity in a naturalised and given human body. Measured against this norm, disabled people are always constituted as other, as deficient and dependent; they will never the able to qualify as competent and able persons.

In the pages that follow, we consider the key aspects of best practice in supporting vulnerable adults online. We make a case for improved policy and pursue how the Cobb ruling can be built on in an inclusive, multi-agency and individual-centric way, to propose that effective support and safeguarding online is not about a 'one size fits all' response in applying recommendations, as implied by the Cobb rulings. In drawing learning from the far more strongly established child online safeguarding world, we look at the role of technology in safeguarding, what works, how it can be empowering, and when it can be excessive. For example, while location tracking could be of value in providing a sense of safety and security to an individual with dementia who has a tendency to wander and get lost, in that they might be able to have fewer physical restrictions if they have consented to being tracked (similar to the argument set out by Ling, 2001 in relation to children's geographic freedom), the non-consensual tracking of a vulnerable adult where their right to privacy was withdrawn in order to 'make sure they are safe' would be highly problematic. This chapter explores the flaws in the dominance of protectionist discourses and builds on Chapters 2 and 5 regarding technological approaches to filtering and monitoring and, again, raises their usefulness as tools while warning against excessive use. Finally, in providing a counter-narrative, the chapter returns to one of the book's central messages – that there is not a universal approach to the effective, respectful safeguarding of vulnerable adults when it comes to online behaviours. There are many threats to the well-being of people with learning disabilities and social connectedness is an important factor in well-being (Cameron and Matthews, 2017). People with learning disabilities experience significantly reduced opportunities to connect with others (Hatton Glover et al, 2016).

As such, in our consideration of online safeguarding and *what works* we strive to ensure that the risk of social exclusion experienced by so many adults with a learning disability is not further unnecessarily compounded by digital exclusion.

> Social exclusion is a complex and multi-dimensional process. It involves the lack or denial of resources, rights, goods and services, and the inability to participate in the normal relationships and activities, available to the majority of people in a society, whether in economic, social, cultural or political arenas. It affects both the quality of life of individuals and the equity and cohesion of society as a whole. (Levitas et al, 2007: 36)

As digital divides based

> on social inequalities drive low levels of access and skills to use the internet; those who are socially excluded are less likely to use the internet and benefit from the internet applications that may help them tackle their exclusion and digital exclusion has the potential to

exacerbate social exclusion e.g. in terms of poor educational attainment and some studies have shown a positive effect of digital participation on indicators of social exclusion. (Martin et al, 2016: 28)

The main factors which shape inclusion are individual characteristics, informal networks, professional care, neighbourhood characteristics (which we suggest include the online neighbourhood) and government policies (Overmars-Marx et al, 2014). According to Power and Bartlett (2018: 565), 'cultivating "inclusion" stands as one of the cornerstones of learning disability policy alongside the other general principles of disability rights: participation, non-discrimination, equality, and accessibility' (UN Convention on the Rights of People with Disabilities 2006).

As we have set out in previous chapters, safeguarding is a well-established responsibility for the social care sector but online safeguarding has only recently become recognised. Online harms are well acknowledged in the compulsory educational sector and exemplified by the Ofsted inspection framework (2018) and the Department for Education's (DfE, 2018) *Keeping Children Safe in Education: Statutory Guidance for Schools and Colleges*. However, such harms do not necessarily cease when young people enter into late adolescence and early adulthood. Introduced in 2017, the Quality Matters initiative aims to improve the quality of adult social care. In order to improve the quality of such care, consideration of supportive networks to enable online participation is required. The Care Act statutory guidance defines adult safeguarding as

> [p]rotecting an adult's right to live in safety, free from abuse and neglect. It is about people and organisations working together to prevent and stop both the risks and experience of abuse or neglect, while at the same time making sure that the adult's wellbeing is promoted including, where appropriate, having regard to their views, wishes, feelings and beliefs in deciding on any action. This must recognise that adults sometimes have complex interpersonal relationships and may be ambivalent, unclear or unrealistic about their personal circumstances.

Best practice requires cognisance of individual capacity issues, online risk, and risk mitigation. 'Dis/ability is about specific passages between equally specific arrays of heterogeneous materials. It is about the character of the materials which en/able those passages. And it is about the arrays which secure or don't secure them – like absent lifts' (Moser and Law, 1999: 201). We draw on Abrams and Gibson's (2017: 346) work adopting ANT as a lens through which disability is viewed 'as a sociomaterial assemblage, a site of network connectivity, rather than an immutable attribute of problem bodies'. This helps to promote understanding of the unique complexity of each individual's capabilities, agency and supportive, facilitating factors as ANT describes actors as an association of a myriad of little elements – human and non-human (see, for example, Gomart and Hennion, 1999). As such, in this chapter, we make the case for up-to-date professional knowledge and a respectful safeguarding approach constantly mindful of the best interests of the individual.

A theoretical framework in understanding 'what works'

As we have already stated, as authors we have nearly 40 years' combined experience of online safeguarding and of what works well, starting with our work in relation to understanding online risk and childhood (Bond, 2010; 2012; 2013; 2014; Bond and Rawlings, 2017; Phippen, 2016). Drawing on empirical evidence of what has been learned in relation to what works to effectively manage risk online it is also important to articulate the theoretical underpinnings of such approaches. We embrace a 'what works' approach, based on Pawson and Tilley's (1997) manifesto on realistic evaluation in that in order to be useful for decision makers, evaluations need to identify *what works, in what circumstances and for whom*, rather than simply claiming that something *works*.

Iterations of ANT, including our own, share a common view that the world consists of shifting networks composed of both human and non-human *actors*. Focusing on ANT showing and telling disability, for example Moser and Law's *Good Passages, Bad Passages* (1999), the theory is useful to understanding the complexity of the relationship between the individual, technology and society in that

> [a]ctor network theory is a form of relational materialism that codifies a body of ideas developed in sociology and history of technology. At is centre is a non-dualistic account of the relation between 'society' and 'technology'. In this view society is produced through the mutually constituting interaction of a wide variety of human and non-human entities (including machines and technologies). (Prout, 1996: 198)

ANT is especially helpful to our analysis here. In Latour's (1993) approach to modernity as a form of belonging, guaranteed through excluding certain characters (hybrids), ANT dissolves boundaries imposed to bring the 'other' back into belonging and endorses democracy (Strathern, 1999). As Abrams and Gibson (2017: 472) observe, ANT helpfully 'decentres the subject and examines what dynamic networks do in their specificity, for example, how they may be both disabling and enabling in different ways in different contexts'. This provides a bespoke account of each unique case, including the enabling (supportive) actors and the disabling (risky) actors in the network for careful consideration. Following Michel Callon and Vololona Rabeharisoa's (2004) *Gino's Lesson on Humanity*, Abrams and Gibson (2017) ask what kind of humanity is put to work in clinical assessment measures. Best-interest assessors should ensure the rights and freedoms of people with learning disabilities are addressed (Watt and Brazier, 2009) and if mental capacity assessments place based on humanitarian rather than protectionist principles at the centre of each assessment, we may see alternative discourses emerging which lead to very different and more inclusive participatory outcomes for those individuals being assessed.

As Galis (2011: 825) eloquently argues,

ANT enables the ordering of disability as a simultaneous biological, material and semiotic phenomenon. The focus of the analysis shifts from merely defining disability as an impairment, handicap, or social construction (epistemology) to how disability is experienced and enacted in everyday practices, in policy-making, in the body, and in the built environment (ontology). This adoption of an ontological approach to disability allows the analysis to not only discuss how disability is done, but also to follow how disability groups and carriers of disability expertise and experience intervene in policy-making by developing 'research in the wild' and confronting scientific experts in different fora (ontological politics).

Risk

Over the past 10 years or so the concept of risk has been central to safeguarding agendas for children and for adults considered vulnerable or 'at risk'. Adult protection has become an issue of central concern for UK service providers and policy makers alike, with governmental publications outlining adult protection guidelines for England (*No Secrets* (Department of Health, 2000) and *Safeguarding Adults* (Association of Directors of Social Services, 2005)) and legislative changes in the Sexual Offences Act 2003 (UK Government, 2003), which introduced increased sentences for those who engage a person who does not have 'capacity to consent' in a sexual act (Hollomotz, 2011). Of course these documents were superseded by the Care Act 2014 (UK Government, 2014), as we have discussed previously. However, they are worthwhile historical documents to consider because they highlight the nature of policy guidance in this area and how, with a dearth of guidance, the vaccum is filled with opinion and value bias. The point we make is that prior to 2000, there was no guidance around capacity to consent. The Mental Capacity Act Code of Practice (2007), is approaching 15 years old and while there are suggestions of updates, they are still not forthcoming. And while the Care Act, in 2014, updated our approach and understanding around safeguarding adults in general, there is scant consideration of capacity to engage with the internet and social media. This is why we are now so reliant upon the Court of Protection and its judgments to try to develop our understanding around 'best practice' regarding capacity to engage with the internet and social media, and where deprivation of liberty is justified in the best interests of the individual.

Online risk, as we have already identified, has only more recently come to dominate safeguarding discourses as Lough and Fisher (2016) observe, with internet use often taking place with little or ill-informed support, meaning that people with learning disabilities might be vulnerable to becoming victims of online crime and/or grooming. Ramsten et al (2019) demonstrated that concerns about internet use are prevalent among family members, carers or supporters of people with learning disabilities. As such the dominance of cyberdistopian understandings have become symptomatic of Beck's *Risk Society* thesis, which underpins our understandings of the digital society in that '[i]n advanced modernity the social production of wealth is systematically accompanied by the social production of risks. Accordingly, the problems and conflicts relating to distribution in a society of scarcity overlap with the problems and conflicts that arise from the production, definition and distribution of techno-scientifically produced risks' (Beck, 1992: 19).

So we have a conflict between guidance for professionals that is old and drawn from a pre-social media era now being used to make judgements on the capacity of individuals to engage with the broad term of 'internet and social media', and emerging literature from the last 10 years that begins to explore the role of online harms for adults who might be at risk. Little wonder, therefore, that practitioners fall back upon personal experience when making decisions around safeguarding. While the child online safeguarding world is awash with statutory guidance, the same cannot be said for safeguarding vulnerable adults.

The culture of risk avoidance in organisations has arisen from the fear of criticism regulators (Tindall, 2015), and an 'over-emphasis by professionals on the level of risk posed to themselves and others by their lifestyle choices' dominates online safeguarding practices (Ottmann et al, 2016: 509). However, just as safety is something socially constructed and subjective (Barnett, 2019: 12), risk is also a social and cultural construction (Beck, 1992). As such the 'perception of 'risk' is predicted on cultural, social and historical factors' (Grosvenor et al, 2009: 1). Therefore, understanding and responding to risk needs to be considered in the wider societal context. This is important in successfully managing risk. The risk of sexual violence, for example, against adults with learning difficulties is shaped by social processes (Hollomotz, 2011) and, as we have outlined earlier in this book, it is clear that responding to online risk in relation to vulnerable adults there are complex relationships which need to be considered. Caton and Landman (2020: 2), for example, suggest that research in this area has 'highlighted a discrepancy between the views of young people with learning disabilities and their parents and/or professionals who work to support them'. Stevens and Hassett (2007: 136) have previously suggested that the complex relationships in risk analyses can be helpfully understood through the sociological approaches to the risk society 'that supports complexity concepts such a dissipative systems and working at the edge of chaos'.

In individualised society, qualitatively, new types of personal risk arise and today's risk derives from internal decisions that depend simultaneously on scientific and social construction: 'the social effect of risk definitions if therefore not dependent on their scientific validity' (Beck, 1992: 32). There is a complex spectrum of online risk associated with adults with a learning disability, as discussed in our earlier chapters and exemplified in the emerging discourses from the Court of Protection rulings, with responsibilities for risk management impacting on organisations and professionals alike. Individualisation, central to Beck's (1992) *Risk Society* thesis, is also a central tennet of the Care Act 2014 (UK Government, 2014) and also important to understanding the concept of *vulnerability* (Phippen and Bond, 2020). It is clear from our previous work that it is the concept of *vulnerability* that underpins the drive for protection in relation to perceptions of children and online risk and it is that same concept that drives the protectionist discourses when responding to adults with a learning disability or reduced mental capacity and risks online. Yet, as we have argued elsewhere, vulnerability is not a static concept and vulnerabilities are diverse (Phippen and Bond, 2020).

What works: organisations

Recently I had contact in England with a woman with learning disabilities who wanted to find a boyfriend through social media. She was very skilled at using dating sites on her smart phone to find men wanting to meet her. Several times a week, she travelled to meet them, or the men came to her home. Occasionally, she alleged the men had sexually assaulted her and went to the police. She was frequently disappointed the sex did not lead to a relationship lasting more than a few days. Those supporting her appropriately cautioned her about the risks of what she was doing. Her response was a very reasonable question – how else was she to get a boyfriend? She had no social networks outside of social media. Questions were asked whether her access to the internet should be stopped. (Thompson, 2019: 21)

Sadly, this eloquent quote from Thompson (2019) is far from unusual and, as illustrated throughout this book, we are aware of far too many examples of how responses to risk are met with prevention responses which are restrictive – even in some cases punitive – rather than supportive. If we adopt a social constructivist perspective on risk as outlined earlier in the chapter, we can see how this woman's experience powerfully illustrates how risk does not simply arise from the woman's behaviour online, but also from what Thompson (2019: 21) describes as 'the failure of those of us who support people with learning disabilities to provide helpful support on using the internet to meet intimate needs'.

Safeguarding processes have created a climate of liability avoidance, with providers striving to reduce their exposure to criticism if something goes wrong (Tindall, 2015). And while the Deprivation of Liberty Safeguards can broadly be welcomed as providing further protection for all vulnerable adults, many of whom will have learning disabilities, there is a lack of certainty surrounding definitions, and staff in all care environments will need to be aware of, identify and prevent possible deprivation of liberty situations (Sergeant, 2009). Rather than adopting a narrow and restricted view of risk management, we argue that effective safeguarding that respects and enables online participations can only be achieved through a holistic approach and an understanding of the complexity of risk. As Power and Bartlett (2018: 567) also propose,

> [m]ore broadly, our research suggests that shedding light on the difficult realities of the peoples, places, and communities who are supposed to become inclusive of people with learning disabilities (who rarely approximate the ideal envisaged in the policy rhetoric) offers a helpful way to critically engage with such debate. A more honest appraisal of impairment effects and a greater appreciation of the 'messiness' of inclusion work on the ground would go a long way to ensure better support is made available to people with learning disabilities in their individual management of their lives in and around their communities.

Thus, in our consideration of the networks that construct risk (Bond, 2014), it is important to remember that it is through *spaces* and *places* that the social is constructed in the negotiation of relations and mulitiplicities (Massey, 2005). Cresswell (2004: 11) proposes that 'place is also a way of seeing, knowing and understanding the world. When we look at the world of places we see different things. We see attachment and connections between people and place.' Power and Bartlett's (2018: 563) study adopts a geographical lens to critically assess people with learning disabilities' own everyday place-based experiences in their efforts to cultivate inclusion through 'the real, on-the-ground, often complex work required by people to create more inclusive lives in the community'.

This is, therefore, an essential concept in our analyses and approaches to safeguarding. For example, when we look at *place* in relation to living arrangements for adults with learning disabilities or mental capacity issues in the UK a very diverse picture emerges. It is clear from research, for example Ottmann et al (2016: 61), that people with a learning disability rely on disability services professionals or informal carers when devising or deploying safeguarding strategies and that '[i]f resourced to do so, family carers, disability support services, and professionals in primary health care are well placed to assist people with intellectual disabilities to devise individualised safeguards that help them not only to "walk from trouble"' but also to stay safe within an everyday life context.

There is a huge diversity in individuals' support networks, ranging from professional disability services and social care support to less formal care from family and friends. Furthermore, these landscapes of support are changing. According to Public Health England (2020) the number of adults with learning disabilities getting some form of long-term social care increased from 139,555 in the period 2014–15 to 147,915 in the period 2017–18. Interestingly, in 2017–18 the most common living situation for adults with learning disabilities aged 18–64 years receiving long-term social care support was settled living with family/friends – 48,165 people. In the same period, 29,975 people were living in some form of supported accommodation, 21,145 people in registered care homes, and 16,640 people in tenancies with local authorities, housing associations or registered social landlords. Over the same time period, the number of adults with learning disabilities living in residential care has decreased, while the number of adults with learning disabilities living with family/friends or living in supported accommodation has increased. These different living arrangements construct different networks of both resilience and risk mediated through space and place.

Furthermore, what is starkly evidenced from Public Health England (2020) data is that from 2014–15 to 2017–18 the number of requests for support from new adult clients with learning disabilities increased from 555 in 2014–15 to 1,140 in 2017–18. However, while the number of requests increased, in 2017–18 the most common sequel to a request for support was no services provided: no identified needs, which increased from 220 requests in 2014–15 to 415 requests in 2017–18. The next most common sequels were no services: universal services/signposting (an increase from 30 requests in 2014–15 to 185 requests in 2017–18) and long-term support (which increased from 175 requests in 2014–15 to 185 requests in 2017–18). Many requests for support are either unmet by statutory services or being referred to universal services, resulting in no support for the majority of individuals and a huge diversity in the delivery of support to those individuals in receipt of some support, whether through formal or informal means.

As 'ANT is committed to demonstrating that the elements bound together in a network (including the people are constituted and shaped by their involvement with each other' (Lee and Brown, 1994: 774). It is therefore the relationship and the involvement between the people, for example the individual with a disability, their supportive network (including organisations, policy, knowledge and understanding) and technologies that constitute reality. Taking Cresswell's (2011) argument about place, and if we view the world of places as different things, we have a better and more nuanced picture of the attachments and connections between people and places. Such an approach reveals the network of supportive or unsupportive factors emerging as fundamental to understanding *what works* in relation to safeguarding online.

This is even more challenging in the context of everyday practice in that 'before we consider what the MCA has to say about assessing capacity, it is worth acknowledging that this specific topic raises a considerable amount of anxiety in practice, inasmuch that many practitioners feel unqualified and inadequate to assess capacity' (Graham, 2016: 93). This is certainly true when it comes to assessing capacity for engaging in the digital society. In our examples (among many others we have come across in our research) knowledge, power and trust are accorded to those who *care* for others. In order for the principles of such 'care' to be maintained the rights and wishes of those receiving 'care' need to be upheld and not be silenced in a blanket of control disguised as care. Symptomatic of a moral panic, many intellectually disabled adults are subjected to a paternalistic regime of care, which is especially true in regard to their sexuality (Foley, 2019). In *The History of Sexuality*, Foucault (1978) argues that sexuality is an open and complex historical system, saturated with power, and modern sexuality in particular is constructed according to a conjunction of knowledge and power that disciplines bodies and pleasures. In Foucauldian terms, cultural sexualised texts (for example pornographic materials) act as points of knowledge, power and trust in which sexuality is specified and disciplined (Daskalopoulou and Zanette, 2020: 971). Bates et al (2017) highlight how the value of personal relationships was supposedly enshrined in law by the HM (1998), which states that everyone has the right to a 'private and family life', including marriage, but *Valuing People Now* (Department of Health, 2009) drew attention to the lack of progress.

> Although the importance of promoting social inclusion for individuals with intellectual disabilities (IDs) is acknowledged in the government White Papers Valuing People and Valuing People Now (Department of Health, 2001: 24; Department of Health, 2007: 10), these have not explicitly stated how this should be pursued nor have these papers suggested social media as a potential avenue for inclusion. (White and Forrester-Jones, 2020: 382)

Arguably, therefore, we suggest that little progress has been made, especially in relation to relationships, sexuality and privacy online. A clear example is access to pornography, which 'provides powerful sexual scripts and templates of behaviour for modern sexual subjects in which male and female pleasure is articulated' (Daskalopoulou and Zanette, 2017: 983) and to deny access to sexual scripts is to deny sexual identity and belonging in a sexualised digital society.

According to Barnett (2019: 9),

> [a]n ideal safeguarding world is one in which routine responses to individuals are challenged and questioned on a regular basis, where preventative measures are favoured over protective measures, and where practitioners understand the importance of information sharing, but do not confide this with the responses to the individual who has care and support needs. It is important to share information and to assess the situation and risks to all persons concerns; however, this does not equate to making decisions about a person, for that person, in response to their needs. The Mental Capacity Act provides the framework for this and is an integral part of all safeguarding work that creates personalised responses to the adult concerned.

ANT is useful here in that networked theory is quite simple as it provides a grounded theory approach (Murdoch, 1997) by conceptualising the approach to assessment through a networked lens. A clear example of the complexity of networked relationships in relation disability is provided by Moser and Law (1999) in their case study in which they outline both technology and dis/ability in terms of a set of specificities which are specific because they form the networks of heterogeneous material. They claim that if the networks are in place ability is achieved but if the networks are not in place disability arises. If we apply an ANT approach to safeguarding online, if the networks – human and non-human – are in place, safeguarding is stronger and risk managed but when the networks are not in place safeguarding is weaker and risk is not managed.

However, what is important in this approach is that we must ensure that human rights are included in the networked approach – rights to participation as well as protection. A tension between self-realisation and control has always been a feature of modernity (Giddens, 1990; 1991). In the double-edged sword of modernity (see Giddens, 1990), risk in relation to social networks and social relationships is only part of the complex array of relationships, and mental health and well-being are also understood to be supported and mediated through a network of relationships with human and non-human elements. Yet currently the policy and practice environment is one in which austerity predominates and 'services are experiencing increasing pressure to create efficiency savings and hate crimes towards people with learning difficulties are increasing' (Cluley, 2017: 31).

Adopting a holistic approach

This section explores policy and practice around online safeguarding to argue for a holistic approach through which there is a sound understanding of how policy and practice work together to safeguard vulnerable adults online. In order to achieve this, there needs to be an ongoing reflection of best practice, where knowledge is better shared across the sector and across organisations both statutory and non-statutory. We know that online safeguarding can be effective and supportive when a community-based approach is adopted and that four key aspects are considered: policy; education and training; technology; and practice.

Policy

Macintosh, writing in 2019 on the Scottish Council for Voluntary Organisations (SCVO), observes:

> One of the key issues discussed was the organisational 'attitude' to digital inclusion and the impact this had on individual practitioners. One participant noted that 'Staff often don't do digital because of their own anxieties that they'll get in trouble, or that the person they support will.'
>
> Very few organisations in attendance had policies in place specifically related to digital to provide inclusive and robust safeguarding for staff and individuals using services. One participant noted that 'It seems silly that when the internet can make such a difference to people's lives that they are being isolated from it by the organisations that support them because they don't have the policies or procedures in place, or even the access.'

The purpose of policy and its implementation should be to effectively deliver a culture of best practice around online safeguarding not to control or limit access to the internet and social media. The guiding principles related to online safeguarding that provide the foundation for practice in the organisation.

Organisations should have a well-established and clearly communicated culture across the organisation. Policies and practices are progressive and proactive, and deal with online safeguarding incidents pre-emptively. The policies and practices of incident response consider broader aspects of prevention, such as well-being and resilience. We know from experience that often organisations have policies in place, for example safeguarding, anti-bullying, equality and diversity and so on, but they often neglect to explicitly cover the online environment. Therefore, ensuring that policies are reviewed by a range of stakeholders to consider how this could be included is essential. Any detailed policy should include clear definitions and how concerns should be responded to and by whom, and consideration needs to be given to how stakeholders are made aware of the policy and how it can be applied. A robust policy is informed from multi-stakeholder input, including service users and external stakeholders, with a multi-stakeholder committee regularly reviewing the policy, using data collected by the organisation on incidents.

In safeguarding policies online safeguarding should be included either within the organisation's safeguarding policy or as a standalone 'online safeguarding policy'. The safeguarding policy should be the overarching policy relating to core expectations around online safeguarding. The policy should determine definitions of behaviours, such as online abuse and harassment, image-based abuse, identity fraud and exploitation, and should detail how the organisation will respond to safeguarding concerns. Policies that include image-based abuse (a specific form of online abuse that relates to the non-consensual sharing of indecent or sexual images) should clearly consider the levels of intervention and image-based abuse, thresholds for law enforcement intervention, and victim-centred support for this form of harm. The safeguarding policy should refer to other policies such as bullying, equality and diversity, and data protection and should be informed from multi-stakeholder input, including external stakeholders. Any safeguarding policy should be regularly reviewed by a multi-stakeholder committee using data collected by the organisation on safeguarding incidents.

Organisations need to consider how they manage data on safeguarding issues and how they ensure that data protection practices are compliant with legislation where there may be some conflict between data protection and safeguarding. Data protection policies should include safeguarding concerns, and safeguarding practices should be audited to ensure data protection compliance. It is essential that all those with responsibility for safeguarding are aware of and have received regular training in data protection practices in line with the statutory requirements of the organisation. Detailed data audits by the organisation's data protection officer should be undertaken regularly, with both policy and practice updated as a result. Online safeguarding is often overlooked in consideration of equality, diversity and inclusion yet there may be elements related to hate crime with an online aspect that need to be considered. Specifically, consideration needs to be given to service users with 'protected characteristics' – including age, disability, gender, gender reassignment, marriage and civil partnership, pregnancy and maternity, race and ethnicity, religion or belief, and sexual orientation. Acknowledgement should be made in policies as to how protected characteristics may place some adults at greater risk. Therefore, equality and diversity policies should consider online elements to hate crime in detail and how the organisation responds to them and should have prevention strategies in place through raising awareness of local and national campaigns and education programmes. It should clearly relate online incidents to other policies (such as online safeguarding and anti-bullying) and differentiate those that might incorporate aspects of hate crime, stating why they should be tackled in order to incorporate equality and diversity into hate crime legislation. The policy should also clearly outline when and how to escalate online hate incidents to other agencies (for example police).

It is absolutely essential that the governance structure for online safeguarding is clear and robust. It should detail the staff responsible for governance related to online safeguarding. There should be a clear structure in place that identifies key roles in online safeguarding across the organisation, the named staff members in those roles, and what is expected of them. Clear lines of communication are defined so staff know who to report online safeguarding matters to. This structure should also include external stakeholders from both statutory (for example adult mental health, GPs, police, adult safeguarding) and non-statutory bodies (for example rape crisis, domestic abuse agencies, faith- and race-based support organisations, and the Revenge Porn Helpline). Expectations of external agencies should also be clearly defined, as are lines of communication and when they should be involved in online safeguarding incidents, so that governance can be applied in a consistent manner and link to the local adult safeguarding board where appropriate. Good practice for organisations also would include a staff code of conduct or acceptable usage policy for social media and online platforms. This is becoming more important as social media tools and platforms are increasingly used by organisations providing social care and support. The policy should clearly define expectations of staff behaviour and should be signed by employees. The code of conduct should clearly state the expectations of staff online as well as offline, and the consequences of failing to adhere to these professional expectations and standards. The policy should therefore be detailed in terms of expectations and sanctions. Like the other policies, it should be informed from multi-stakeholder input, including external stakeholders. Stakeholders need to be aware of the code/policy and how it can be applied. The code should be informed by emerging trends and disciplinary data, and should be frequently reviewed and updated.

Education and training

Careful consideration needs to be given to how resources, information and guidance are used to help deliver policy and practice related to online safeguarding and are developed and accessed by organisations. This includes how and which staff are trained to be aware of online safeguarding issues, and what the depth of the training should be, for example, for front line workers or for those with managerial responsibility. What the training covers and how often it is delivered, reviewed and refreshed are also important if it is to be effective. How staff training relates to governance structures also needs exploring. Online safeguarding should not just be viewed as a part of new employees' induction, but updated training delivered regularly for staff with safeguarding responsibilities is essential. Resources should also be made available to all staff so they can update their knowledge as part of CPD and to enable them to be aware of relevant policies and how to respond effectively to online safeguarding incidents.

All safeguarding-related training (for example, Prevent, bystanderism, domestic violence and consent) includes online elements and needs to include how these issues can be mitigated. Training should highlight how online risks can be recognised and how they can be reported, as well as approaches to rectification of harms, such as use of the right to be forgotten. Good practice in training would link with external stakeholders (for example police, adult social care, public health) and would also be delivered by them where necessary.

Staff training should explain the role of internal stakeholders and signpost support from these groups as if staff are made aware of the services offered by internal stakeholders they will understand how these can be appropriately applied in the event of an online safeguarding incident. Specific services might align to different statutory responsibilities (for example Prevent) and other safeguarding incidents that may have an online element (for example domestic violence). Staff need to know when they should report concerns around online risk and harm, and who to report to and if they are aware of the limitations of internal stakeholders, they will know when it is necessary to engage with external bodies, for example the police, in addressing online safeguarding incidents. Staff training should also clearly explain the role of external stakeholders and signpost support from these groups so that staff are made aware of the services offered by external stakeholders and how these can be appropriately applied in the event of an online safeguarding incident. Specific services might be aligned to different statutory responsibilities (for example Prevent) and other safeguarding incidents that may have an online element (for example in cases of domestic violence, coercion and control).

What works best is when staff have single points of contact with external stakeholders (for example the local adult safeguarding board) and can collaboratively work with them to resolve online safeguarding incidents. Inter-professional training is a key aspect to a positive learning experience combined with clear real-life case studies to improve professionals' knowledge and understanding of online safeguarding and improve their confidence in supporting vulnerable adults in their care (see Bond and Dogaru, 2019).

Technology

The role of technology in safeguarding adults online is extensively explored in previous chapters, but it is also important to consider how technological tools used to help deliver policy and practice related to online safeguarding will vary widely between organisations and social care providers. It is essential that in any situation, how the organisation uses tools to monitor internet access across its networks and the use of filtering needs to be clearly communicated and transparent. It is also essential that care should be taken to reflect the nature of the users across networks (that is, generally adult) and the risk of over-blocking legal content. However, the systems should be clear in addressing illegal content (for example using the Internet Watch Foundation's blacklist, Child Abuse Image Content). Technology exists to block illegal content (for example Internet Watch Foundation blacklist) and other 'harmful' content based upon organisational policy, for example the protection of access to terrorist material or materials that might lead into terrorism (as defined in the Counter-Terrorism and Security Act 2015 (UK Government, 2015) but differentiated filtering can be managed based upon the needs of groups of users, and in some cases may be lifted for all but illegal content. Institutional policy should be open and transparent and regularly reviewed and users need to be made aware of the monitoring policy, how and when alerts are raised, and lines of communication in the case of an alert.

Monitoring is different from filtering in that it is proactive and responds to breaches of acceptable use, as defined in the organisation's policies, and users also need to be made aware of clear routes for requesting changes to filtering and monitoring based upon their individual needs. Individualisation is reflected in everyday technology use (Bond, 2014) and as such organisations should have clear policies which define how individuals use organisational technical resources (for example internet access/Wi-Fi) via their own personal devices. Furthermore, with the Internet of Things (IoT) and the increase in technology-assisted devices for disabilities, for example remote access to thermostats, live-streaming surveillance cameras and tracking devices, additional consideration is required to ensure such devices promote and support well-being and do not obsessively monitor or control individuals' freedoms and liberties. A policy should be in place which defines sanctions for abuse carried out using IoT devices related to safeguarding matters and any staff safeguarding training should include issues related to IoT devices and how they can potentially be used for abuse.

Practice

Carpenter et al (2014: 557) observe how 'social workers and other professionals are sometimes faced with taking decisions and acting on behalf of people who lack the capacity to make decisions for themselves' and that 'these people are, by definition, among the most vulnerable to oppression in any society'.

> In any given scenario where there is a response to the person given their health, services or wellbeing, then we must ensure that we are not being overly protective because of our own fears and that we are offering the person the opportunity to take sufficient risks to learn and grow. (Barnett, 2019: 10)

In order to achieve this Ottmann et al (2016: 47) propose that

> [p]eople living with intellectual disabilities have a right to be safe from abuse and neglect and have a right to be included in the decision-making process determining safeguards that will affect them. However, the research evidence that could underpin good professional practice in terms of co-producing safeguards against abuse and neglect directly involving people with intellectual disabilities is largely missing. People living with intellectual disability can and should be directly involved in decisions that aim at keeping them safe. They should have access to both safety training and a supported decision-making process. Safety risk profiles change as people age. Safety training should take this into account.

Service user engagement is therefore absolutely essential to 'what works' in professional practice related to online safeguarding, and service users should be represented at all levels of online safeguarding practice. Effective online safeguarding is essentially a collaborative endeavour between services users, care providers and organisations, with the views and experiences of service users underpinning the development of policy, awareness-raising initiatives and training. While there is little research available on 'what works' in online safeguarding practice, a review of the published literature reveals some encouraging positive examples of effective support. Caton and Landman's (2020) study, for example, found that in a peer education project which considered internet safety specifically about risks of online radicalisation and extremism, the students with a learning disability better understood possible links between grooming and online radicalisation and their teachers simultaneously increased their understanding of the importance of digital engagement for the students. It is well recognised that people with learning difficulties are considerably more likely to experience sexual and other forms of violence than non-disabled people but there is a growing body of research which emphasises that people with a learning disability, with the right support, are active agents in keeping safe and not merely passive recipients of protection from others. Hollomotz (2011) observes how people with learning difficulties have knowledge and understanding of risk and can articulate their right not to be hurt but that they often need help with this, for example when telling a person that they should stop touching them. Hollomotz's (2011) study illustrates that support with keeping safe is very important for people but how when people with a disability ask for help they are not always taken seriously; and, as such, we need to make sure that we listen to people, so that we can help them to stay safe. Furthermore, Leo et al (2018) explore the impact of a social media skills programme on experiences of social inclusion among youth with disabilities, who revealed a more critical and reflective approach to their social media use following the programme. Therefore, all levels of practice related to online safeguarding, including training delivery for staff and help and support for service users, should include awareness raising, with discussions centred on preventing incidents and monitoring effectiveness of strategies proactively as well as reactively.

A key aspect of monitoring the effectiveness of strategies is the reporting of online safeguarding incidents or concerns across the institution and for this to be successful all stakeholders should be aware of the reporting routes. This includes professionals, service users and their friends and families knowing how and where to appropriately report concerns. Information should be regularly updated and mechanisms in place to ensure that information is up to date and reports monitored on an ongoing basis. Reports can be used anonymously (as we have done with the case studies in this book) both to inform new interventions for safeguarding and to increase effectiveness of awareness raising and staff training on an ongoing basis.

Clear, accessible communication about obligations with regard to conduct, acceptable standards of behaviour, and of the likely consequences of failure to meet these obligations for service users and those professionals who care for them is also important in holistic approaches to online safeguarding of vulnerable adults. Furthermore, timely, objective and thorough investigations into allegations of online misconduct, with due regard to confidentiality, are also an important part of this approach, as are effective processes of incident responses with a clearly defined workflow to address serious incidents related to online safeguarding. All staff should be aware of incident response mechanisms depicting a workflow model which defines clear process depending on the nature of the incident and the relationships between offender and victim, with intervention points for referral internally (for example who it should be passed to) and to external agencies (for example when to engage with law enforcement).

Carpenter et al (2014: 591) propose that 'the need to protect the rights of service users who lack capacity to take their own decisions about their care and treatment and to promote their best interests should be at the heart of social work practice'. Safeguarding is everyone's responsibility and we know that 'what works' relies on organisations proactively (not just reactively responding to incidents when they occur) embracing online safeguarding and having service users' views and experiences at the centre of their overall approach. An established culture of actively promoting digital well-being with zero tolerance of online abuse that is clearly and consistently articulated to service users and their carers is fundamental to effective safeguarding alongside a clear governance structure. Successfully fostering a proactive approach also involves raising awareness of online rights and making best use of online and offline channels of communication in a clear and consistent programme of awareness raising and educational initiatives that is regularly updated and evaluated. Such a programme, additionally informed by monitoring, reporting and wider concerns, should cover a range of issues such as revenge porn, indecent images, and coercive control through social media delivered and supported by professionals who have relevant and appropriate training to support adults with learning disabilities to engage in online activities, social media and meaningful participation online.

Additionally, Van Deursen and Van Dijk (2014) outline digital divides and difference in internet skills, building on previous work (see Van Deursen and Van Dijk, 2009) to include operational (basic skills), formal (navigation and orientation), information (user information needs), strategic (capacity to use the internet as a means to reach particular goals and improve position in society), as well as social, creative and mobile skills. Helsper and Van Deursen (2015) add that communication and socio-emotional skills should be included in this framework as these are important skills in the context of social media.

'What works' in four steps

Our sincere thanks goes to James Codling, the Mental Capacity Act and Deprivation of Liberty Safeguards Training and Development Manager from Cambridgeshire County Council's Learning and Development Team for allowing us to reproduce the following recommendations here:

Step 1 – Identify the specific harm and/or risk in relation to the persons internet and social media use

Complete a thorough risk assessment as this is where you need to begin to outline the specific risk/harm issue or issues. Wherever possible this should be done collaboratively with the person. If you were not able to complete this with the person explain why not.

If there is more than one harm and/or risk identified look at them separately, unless there is a very clear overlap between them?

Begin to ask yourself 'what is the actual decision in hand'? In other words if you were going to ask the person how they like to manage this identified risk and or harm *how would you phrase this question to the person*? Remember, if you do not define this question with specific precision at the start, the exercise will be pointless.

Once you have identified the specific decision make a clear record of this in your notes.

Remember at this stage we are not thinking about capacity, start by thinking supported decision making.

Step 2 – What are the planned supportive interventions that you are going to offer the person to manage the identified harm or risk?

This should include:

A brief explanation of why we believe that a supportive intervention is necessary. Your risk assessment should be able to provide you the evidence needed for this conclusion.

Identified the salient and relevant details that the person needs to understand/comprehend (ignoring the peripheral and minor details), at the same time remembering not to set the bar to high.

An outline of what the different supportive interventions could be. This should include exploring doing nothing if this is what the person wants.

What are the potential advantages and disadvantages of the options/ measures and how are you supporting the person to understand this.

How your support has been tailored to the persons specific learning/ support needs (Principle 2, MCA).

Step 3 – Is there any reason to doubt this persons capacity to make their own decisions about how the specific risk or harm is managed?

If the answer is no:

- Have you documented the risks that have been discussed with the person and the reasons why you consider that the person is able and willing to take on those risks?
- Have you clearly recorded the decision that the person has decided to make?
- If people have raised concerns about the persons mental capacity in relation to this matter, may it beneficial to outline your conclusions in a Mental Capacity report.

- Remember, even when the person is able to make the decision this does not stop you offering continued support to the person.

Step 4 – Is there any reason to doubt this persons capacity to make their own decisions about how the specific risk or harm is managed?

If the answer is yes:

- Firstly, ask yourself 'is the problem with me and not with them'? Is the information relevant to the decision clear and accessible, have they got the right support to make the decision, would a different person get a different result, etc.

If you believe that you have done everything practicable to support the persons to make the decision evidence; why you believe that the person could not understand, or retain, or use/weigh the relevant information, or communicate the decision in spite of the assistance given, and why you believe that the inability to make this decision is because of the impairment of the mind or brain.

For detailed guidance on completing mental capacity assessments and reports go to the 39 Essex Chambers mental capacity guidance note and Relevant information for different categories of decision (page 8 to 9).

Step 4 – Should the person lack the capacity to make the decision for themselves, a best interests assessment and decision will need to be made.

This should include (Cont.):

- Whether the person or anyone interested in their welfare is objecting to the proposed best interests decision? If there is an objection this should be immediately discussed with your manager and legal advice may be required.
- Consider whether:
  a. Further education and practicable assistance would make a difference. If you do, you must clearly outline, what the support/ education will include, a timeline for the delivery of that support, outline who will deliver it and why they were chosen and include a review date where the persons decision making / capacity could be re-considered or
  b. Be able to evidence why you believe that no amount of education would change their ability to make this decision for themselves. We would strongly suggest corroborating evidence from either a psychologist or psychiatrist will be needed to evidence this conclusion.

For more detailed guidance refer to the 39 Essex Chambers 'A brief guide Best Interest Assessments'.

What does 'good' look like?

We have throughout this chapter explored what, in our experience, works and also drawn some best practice from a highly experienced practitioner with whom we work. However, as we have stated at various stages throughout this book, this is not a textbox or a flow chart approach to adult online safeguarding. That is because there is no one approach that works best.

We would hope the discussion earlier will both inform the knowledge base around adult online safeguarding and also provide some food for thought for practitioners who have to deal with these disclosures. There is a need, throughout all online safeguarding, to move away from prevention and stopping behaviours, and instead to refocus on how to provide a safe, supportive environment for any at-risk individual to be confident that they can disclose and receive support as a result. We know that many individuals at risk will not disclose because they fear judgement or removal of internet access, and the most important thing for any risk of online harm is that this needs to change.

In the case of adult online safeguarding, 'good' is making evidence-led, informed, victim-centric judgements free from value bias and in the best interests of the individual at risk. There is no piece of technology, video resource or flow chart that can achieve this safeguarding.

Conclusions: a shift towards inclusion?

Power and Bartlett (2018: 565) suggest that the policy goal of *inclusion* is predicated on a person with a learning disability being able to move towards 'a life like any other'. Indeed the concept of inclusion has arguably, according to Power and Barrlett (2018: 563), gained greater international reach in the wake of being enshrined in the general principles of the UNCRPD (Article 3(c): 'full and effective participation and inclusion in society'). This means being able to participate in all the aspects of the community – to work, learn, get about, meet people, be part of social networks, and access goods and services – and to have the support to do so (Department of Health, 2009: 16). However, as we have articulated in this book a climate of *protectionism* and *risk aversion* persists for people with learning disabilities engaging with such online. Although it has been argued that the climate of risk aversion reflects the environment within which service providers operate, it would be more productive for professionals and policy makers to be less critical of providers who have taken all reasonable steps to minimise harm to individuals while upholding their human rights and ability to make decisions and to remember that relationships are a part of human nature, which is unpredictable, and only when this climate of risk aversion reduces can relationships truly flourish (Bates et al 2017).

According to Thompson (2019: 22), 'the internet needs to be understood as an important tool for people with learning disabilities and those who support them to make, develop and retain relationships, whether or not they are sexual'. We are seeing evidence of some shift in that as White and Forrester-Jones (2020: 383) observe, 'the "e-inclusion" movement has developed, with the aim of reducing the disparity of access and usage of information and communication technologies among different sectors of society'. But this goal centres on a commitment that people with learning disabilities are supported to participate and become empowered citizens (Power and Bartlett, 2018). In order to do so 'people living with "intellectual disabilities" should not only have access to comprehensive, life course-focused safety training, but they also should also be directly engaged in deliberations and decision-making processes around safeguarding and risk management that are grounded in everyday life' (Ottmann et al, 2016: 61). As ANT lets us recast disability as an outcome of material and social relations in that disabled bodies cohere as such only in wider networks, where personhood is evolved through specific material techniques and as such a disabled personhood emerges through actor–network interactions, such interactions can support overcoming the limitations of or barriers imposed on a disabled personhood (Abrams and Gibson, 2017).

This chapter, although intentionally not exhaustive, has touched on concepts of citizenship, rights, participation and protection in consideration of the digital society and intellectual disability. The MCA 2005 provided a strong focus for change and for safeguarding to become more person centred (Barnett, 2019: 44). Digital citizenship is central to empowerment and equality in contemporary digital and network society (Castells, 2010), and therefore we urgently need to address 'democratic participation, citizenship and identity' (Fussey and Roth, 2020: 671) in digital society for adults with an intellectual disability. Reflecting on our extensive research practice in relation to online risk and online vulnerability, it is clear that the dominant discourses from child protection online have overshadowed the debates on online participation for some adults also. Yet according to Koubel (2016) one of the key messages from the DoH 2009 consultation was that safeguarding adults is not like child protection and that safeguarding must be built on empowerment and listen to the victim's voice. There is an intricate and mutually constitutive relationship between the human and the technical (Prout, 1996). Everyone has a responsibility to empower individuals – to help with options, information and support, and enable them to retain control to make or be assisted to make their own choices – and the participation or representation of people who lack capability for whatever reason is vital when making decisions about people's safety (Koubel, 2016).

Although there appear to be some potential risks of using social networking sites, there are also many benefits for people with learning disabilities using them as well. The networking sites offer service users the opportunity to expand their social circle and keep in contact with others on a regular basis. Like so many other people, it also offers people with learning disabilities a chance to make their thoughts and opinions known in an environment, which they may feel they have more control over. It is therefore important to get the balance right, offering people with learning disabilities the same rights and freedom as everyone else, whilst ensuring that we can empower them to deal with any difficulties they experience online. (Holmes and O'Loughlin, 2012: 7)

According to McLaughlin (2020: 399), 'the disability movement, particularly in the UK, has long argued that institutionalised models of "care" are central pillars in the oppression of disabled people'. Furthermore, Rogers (2016: 5) argues that the dominance of 'normalcy' and discourses of tolerance have 'been woven into legislation and cultural perceptions of 'abnormality''. While we strive towards person-centred emancipatory practice in a culture of care (Graham, 2016), 'intellectually disabled people are stigmatised' and in a care ethics model of disability, care is not about control and can encompass risk taking (Rogers, 2016: 140). It is interesting that while 'the desire for safety and security has become one of the ways we justify ownership of the [mobile] device' (Ling, 2012: 116), yet reflecting the double-edged sword of modernity (Giddens, 1990), it is simultaneously viewed as a threat to safety and security for adults with an intellectual disability. However, simply denying or allowing access through controlling technology also falls into deterministic trappings of cybertopian or cybersceptic discources and fails to acknowledge the complexity of self-identity, inclusion, and intimacy and sexuality, among other fundamental human rights, in late modernity.

No matter how much we want to make safeguarding a simple matter, decision making will always be as complex as human beings are. Put human beings with other human beings and the complexities increase. Ascribe roles, titles and powers to certain people and the issues are further complicated by the interaction between people. Place each group of people within a different area of society with differing demographics and the possibilities, differences and complexities are infinite. The possible definitions of safe and feeling safe alone would be vastly different. (Barnett, 2019: 285)

8

Some conclusions

In this book we have explored the challenges around the online safeguarding of vulnerable adults, with a focus on those with learning difficulties which may present capacity challenges when engaging with online services. We aimed to address a large gap in the knowledge base around online safeguarding – how we support vulnerable adults. We refer again here, as we did in the introductory chapter, to John Law:

> Something like this seems to happen: first the dispossessed have no voice at all. Then, when they start to create a voice, they are derided. Then, (I am not sure of the order), they are told that they are wrong, or they are told that this was something that everyone knew all along. Then they are told that they are in danger. Then finally, in a very partial form, it may be that their voices are heard and taken seriously. And it has been a struggle all the way. (Law, 1991: 2)

While there is a broad policy history and academic literature around online safeguarding, the vast majority of the knowledge base focuses upon children and young people. As with many aspects of social care, it would seem, post 18, that individuals are left to their own devices and we hope for the best. Similarly, we see legislation that is a patchwork of, arguably, afterthoughts and filling in the gaps, rather than any focused effort to consider a holistic approach to the online safeguarding of vulnerable adults.

While the best interests focus of the MCA 2005 demonstrated a revolution in mental health law that aligned legislation with the rights of the individual and an assumption that a person has capacity unless it is *proved* otherwise, it is arguably not the case that this proof is particularly rigorous in some practice and the judgements of professionals. This is perhaps demonstrated most starkly with online harms. We have, throughout this book, presented many case examples where the best interests of the individual were ignored while a prohibitive approach was chosen, presumably because it provided an easier solution for those with caring responsibilities. We acknowledge the challenges of applying the MCA to modern online behaviours and discourse. There are challenging behaviours and a need to make judgements on capacity of online engagement that could not have been envisaged in 2005 when the Act received royal assent.

One of the reasons for the establishment of the Court of Protection was to allow the Act to form a foundation for judgements that arise from challenges around mental capacity. As such, Court of Protection rulings provide us with an evidence base for the thinking around capacity judgements and build upon the established legislation. Within this exploration we have used the ground-breaking [2019] EWCOP 2 and [2019] EWCOP 3 Cobb J rulings regarding capacity to engage 'the internet and social media' as a starting point for our analysis of how the legal world around safeguarding those adults with capacity issues has progressed its thinking. These rulings present a new direction in Court of Protection decisions, which laid the foundations for those working with, and considering the rights of, adults with learning difficulties and how they engage with online services and, if necessary, when and how capacity decisions are made. In Cobb J's judgment, the definition of six 'rules' that allow professionals to make an assessment of the potential for capacity challenges regarding engaging with online services present a basis for future decision making. It was clear from the rulings that these rules were presented as guidance, something to start a conversation regarding the potential for challenges around capacity to engage. However, in our own assessment of the rules, while they are sound in thinking and definition, there is a risk that the bar will be set higher for those with learning difficulties or capacity challenges compared to the rights of those without these issues for engaging with online services. As we have discussed throughout this book, we would imagine many without capacity issues would struggle to pass all of Cobb J's tests.

Since the Cobb J rulings, there have been a number of Court of Protection rulings, discussed in this book, that have moved the legal thinking about capacity to engage with 'the internet and social media' forward. In our exploration of these rulings we have see both progressive and challenging thinking around these issues, in particular evidence of perhaps an enthusiasm to demonstrate lack of capacity because it is 'easier' than considering best interests and how risk mitigation might be put in place. We have also seen conjecture presented as fact by some with caring responsibilities, and a clear lack of knowledge on the part of expert witnesses. Equally, we have seen clear, best-interest-focused judgements that do not look for easy answers and encourage a focus on the individual. One of our fundamental issues with capacity to engage with 'the internet and social media' – simply that this is far too broad a term to use in such a binary choice – is slowly being eroded and [2021] EWCOP 20, where Williams J explored this in depth, is, in our view, one of the most important rulings to have emerged from the Court of Protection and one that merits much consideration by professionals. One does not simply have capacity to use the internet and social media; there might be many aspects in which one is capacitious, however there might be others that, as a result of vulnerability or disability, in which they might not. To withdraw any access to digital technology to address a specific risk seems hardly in the best interests of the individual.

The motivation for this book came from our own work with professionals and their feedback, and growing frustrations with the dearth of literature to support professionals supporting individuals with mental capacity issues. We have, through our work with safeguarding professionals, seen many who are working to do their best to support individuals in their care, without underpinning knowledge or support from managers to obtain training in order to develop it. They are faced with vulnerable individuals who are engaging in practices with which they are not familiar, or even with which they disagree, and perhaps the only knowledge they bring to the judgements they need to make are their own personal experiences in the online world. This is not a solid foundation upon which to support vulnerable individuals. Furthermore, we see professionals who want straightforward *solutions* to ensure those they care for are free of harm. A noble wish, but one that is challenging if one understands the nature of online harm. As explored in Chapter 2, and as reinforced within Cobb J's rulings, the dearth of knowledge around the online safeguarding of vulnerable adults has resulted in them turning to the child online safeguarding world for guidance. There is a risk that the protectionist and prohibitive discourses that dominate the child safeguarding world might be repeated within adults' safeguarding, and that we miss the opportunity to rethink online safeguarding in an individualistic and rights-based manner.

In particular, as we can see in the emergent Online Safety Bill, online safeguarding has a tendency to turn to technology to provide those with caring responsibilities with the tools to prevent harms. And sadly, the political discourse over the last 10 years has focused almost entirely on technological intervention, leaving behind the need for multiple stakeholder engagement from informed, well-trained stakeholders. In the same way that brakes and bumpers on a car cannot prevent all road harms, technology will never ensure safety online.

As explored throughout this book, even the term online safety implies an unachievable goal. By using this term we are presenting policy makers and professionals with an ideal that will never be achieved and a mindset of prevention rather than empowerment and risk mitigation. If we achieve safety, we will not have to worry about harm. This is simply not possible in the online world. In the same way that we cannot ensure harm-free living in the offline world, it is not possible with online interactions because, in their essence, online systems are simply reflections of the offline world – they provide individuals with the means to access information, to communicate with others, to shop, to consume content, and to be entertained. If we cannot eradicate abuse from the 'real' world, how can we hope to do so with its online mirror?

We can, however, equip individuals to mitigate that risk, if we understand these risks and how to mitigate them. We will not learn this by making demands on providers to prevent harms and bringing in legislation to make a geographical nation the 'safest' part of a global interconnected system. Technology can play an essential role in safeguarding – it can provide the tools to recognise abuse, to allow those being subject to abuse to report it and be supported, and it can provide the means for individuals to prevent abusers from contact or interacting with them. It cannot, however, automate the eradication of harm and also has the potential, with its promises of safety, to distort safety into control. While there might be a view that if we monitor an individual and prevent them from accessing anything harmful, surely we can ensure they are safe and free from harm. And while some rights to privacy might have a legitimate challenge in the need to ensure safety, that should be done for specific risks and potential harms, not the blanket removal of any rights because 'if we can see what you're doing, we can make sure you're safe'. Modifying the stakeholder model we presented in Chapter 2, we present a broad proposition around the online safeguarding of vulnerable adults that challenges protectionist discourses. All of the stakeholders in the model have responsibilities, and it is through their interaction that the best interests of the individual can be supported. This is not a case of hoping someone else can address a risk or harm, it is about working together to achieve this and being mindful of the role each stakeholder has to play to support the individual. We also bring in past behaviours and learning by the individual being brought to their own online behaviours. Vulnerable adults do not come to the attention of social care services without any previous experiences online. They bring with them their own experiences, potential past harms, learning from educational settings, and so on, which all contribute to their view of the online world. Stakeholders need to be mindful of this and work with them. We also need to be mindful that vulnerability is not a static concept. An individual might become vulnerable as a result of circumstance or behaviour – it does not mean they are always vulnerable, or they will be vulnerable in the future. They are, however, vulnerable at a given time and require support that is mindful of their rights and informed by knowledge of the online world and the associated legal thinking.

We hope this book provides a thought-provoking discussion for those who study vulnerability, and those who work with adults who are vulnerable. We have not aimed to provide a 'to do' guide because there is no guide that would work for all individuals in all scenarios. Each case needs to be judged on its merits, with the MCA and its underlying principles as the starting

Figure 8.1: Stakeholder model for adult online safety

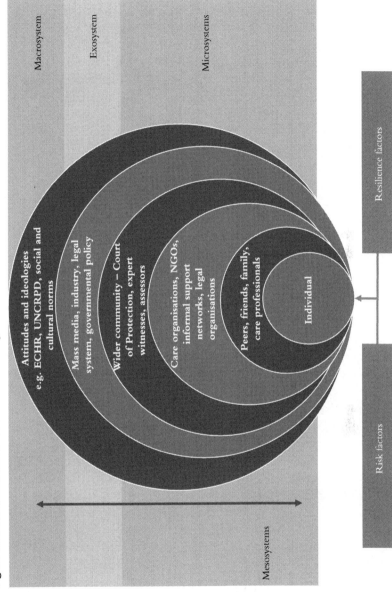

Source: Authors, based on Bronfenbrenner (1979)

point to consider what is best for the individual. However, there are some things that might make the lives of those who care for the vulnerable, and the vulnerable themselves, easier.

First, as we have discussed at length in this book, there is a need to unpick the patchwork and bring in specific legislation that considers the online safeguarding of vulnerable adults. We note, at the time of writing, that the Online Safety Bill, the piece of legislation, we are told, that will make the UK the 'safest place to go online in the world', makes no mention whatsoever of vulnerable adults. Providers have duties towards children and adults. Once again, vulnerable adults, who probably fit in to the 'too hard' box with this type of regulatory approach, are not considered specifically. This needs to change and legislation with specific focus on the best interests of vulnerable adults and their online safeguarding needs to be developed so that those who care for them are clear on the legal position and feel supported by it. Within any such legislation there is a clear need to support those who work with vulnerable adults to be properly equipped, with effective training and support from management, so that they can understand the issues those in their care face, and how they might best mitigate risk. We have seen throughout this book the complexity of some of the cases care professionals have to face. This is not something that they should be addressing without formal professional development. Having social experiences with digital technology does not mean one is equipped to tackle complex online safeguarding scenarios and we have seen plenty of examples of value bias being brought into in this arena as a result.

And clearly there is also a role for technology providers. However, that role is not to stop online harms from happening because if this is what we expect, we are always doomed to fail. Technology can do much, and there is certainly more that can be done. Some elements of the Online Safety Bill, such as demonstrable risk assessment and transparency reporting – showing the sorts of reports they deal with, and how they deal with them – are to be welcomed. However, probably because vulnerable adults were not considered when the Bill was drafted, there is more that is not in it. For example, routes for disclosure by third parties, which would allow someone with caring responsibility to raise concern with the platform without the need to invade the individual's privacy, would be a positive step. So would supporting education programmes for individuals and care professionals. Education is another aspect of safeguarding that is notably lacking from the Bill.

What is clear is there are no easy solutions to these issues, and they are not going to go away. Technology will advance, new exciting ways of interacting online will evolve, and with it new risks and potential harms. And technology alone cannot prevent these harms from occurring.

References

Abrams, T. and Gibson, B. E. (2017) 'Putting Gino's Lesson to Work: Actor–Network Theory, Enacted Humanity, and Rehabilitation', *Health* Vol. 21 (4) pp 425–40 doi:10.1177/1363459315628039

American Academy of Paediatrics (2016) *American Academy of Paediatrics Announces New Recommendations for Children's Media Use* https://www.aap.org/en-us/about-the-aap/aap-press-room/pages/american-academy-of-pediatrics-announces-new-recommendations-for-childrens-media-use.aspx

American Psychological Association *Increasing Access and Coordination of Quality Mental Health Services for Children and Adolescents* http://www.apa.org/about/gr/issues/cyf/child-services.aspx

Association of Directors of Social Services (2005) *Safeguarding Adults A National Framework of Standards for good practice and outcomes in adult protection work* https://www.adass.org.uk/adassmedia/stories/publications/guidance/safeguarding.pdf

Bardone-Cone, A. M. and Cass, K. M. (2006) 'Investigating the Impact of Pro-Anorexia Websites: A Pilot Study', *European Eating Disorders Review* Vol. 14 pp 256–62.

Barnett, D. (2019) *The Straightforward Guide to Safeguarding Adults: From Getting the Basics Right to Applying the Care Act and Criminal Investigations.* London: Jessica Kingsley.

Bates, C., Terry, L. and Popple, K. (2017) 'Supporting People with Learning Disabilities to Make and Maintain Intimate Relationships', *Tizard Learning Disability Review* Vol. 22 (1) pp 16–23.

BBC News (2019a) *WhatsApp 'Snake Porn' Prosecution Questioned by Judge* https://www.bbc.co.uk/news/uk-england-bristol-48379744

BBC News (2019b) *Christchurch Shootings: Sajid Javid Warns Tech Giants Over Footage* https://www.bbc.co.uk/news/uk-47593536

BBC News (2019c) *How Can You Stop Your Kids Viewing Harmful Web Content?* https://www.bbc.co.uk/news/business-47853554

BBC News (2021) *Robyn Williams: Sacked Met Officer Wins Appeal Against Dismissal* https://www.bbc.co.uk/news/uk-england-london-57501764

Beck, U. (1992) *Risk Society Towards a New Modernity.* London: Sage.

Berryman, C., Ferguson, C. J. and Negy, C. (2018) 'Social Media Use and Mental Health among Young Adults', *Psychiatric Quarterly* Vol. 89 pp 307–14.

Bhatia, S. and Tingle, R. (2020) 'Coroner Records Suicide Verdict on Death of Tory MP Owen Paterson's Wife, 63, Who Hanged Herself After Leaving No Note and Having Made Plans to Meet Family', *The Daily Mail*, 22 September, https://www.dailymail.co.uk/news/article-8759579/Owen-Patersons-wife-63-hanged-woodland-near-family-home.html

Bond, E. (2010) 'The Mobile Phone = Bike Shed? Children, Sex and Mobile Phones', *New Media & Society* Vol. 13 (4) pp 587–604.

Bond, E. (2012) *Virtually Anorexic – Where's the Harm?* https://www. thechildrensmediafoundation.org/wp-content/uploads/2014/02/Bond-2012-Research-on-pro-anorexia-websites.pdf

Bond, E. (2013) 'Mobile Phones, Risk and Responsibility: Understanding Children's Perceptions', *CyberPsychology: Journal of Psychosocial Research on Cyberspace* Vol. 7 (1).

Bond, E. (2014) *Childhood, Mobile Technologies and Everyday Experiences.* Basingstoke: Palgrave.

Bond, E. (2018) 'Demonising Discourses: Delving into the Debate. Conflict and Context in the Image of the Ultra-thin Body Pro-ana – A Different View from Rhetoric to Responsibility', *Entertainment Law Review* Vol. 29 (1) pp 3–6.

Bond, E. and Dogaru, C. (2019) 'An Evaluation of an Inter-Disciplinary Training Programme for Professionals to Support Children and Their Families Who Have Been Sexually Abused Online', *The British Journal of Social Work* Vol. 49 (3) pp 577–94 https://doi.org/10.1093/bjsw/bcy075

Bond, E. and Phippen, A. (2019a) 'Teaching Online Safety in School Guidance – New Non-Statutory Guidance from the Department for Education Leaves Much to be Desired', *Entertainment Law Review* Vol. 30 (8) pp 244–6.

Bond, E. and Phippen, A. (2019b) 'Why Is Placing the Child at the Centre of Online Safeguarding So Difficult?', *Entertainment Law Review* Vol. 30 (3) pp 80–4.

Bond, E. and Rawlings, V. (2017) 'Virtual Vulnerability – Safeguarding Children in Digital Environments' in Dastbaz, M, Arabnia, H. and Aghkar, B (eds.) *Technology and Smart Futures.* London: Springer.

Borzekowski, D. L. G., Schenk, S., Wilson, J. L. and Peebles, R. (2010) 'e-Ana and e-Mia: A Content Analysis of Pro-eating Disorder Websites', *American Journal of Public Health* Vol. 100 (8) pp 1526–34.

Boyd, D., Ryan, J. and Leavitt, A. (2011) 'Pro-Self-Harm and the Visibility of Youth-Generated Problematic Content' in *I/S: A Journal of Law and Policy for the Information Society* Vol. 7 (1) pp 1–32, www.danah.org/papers/2011/IS-ProSelfHarm.pdf

Boyle, J. (2017) 'Foucault in Cyberspace: Surveillance, Sovereignty, and Hardwired Censors' in Berryman, P. S. (ed.) *Law and Society Approaches to Cyberspace.* London: Routledge.

Branley, D. B. and Covey, J. (2017) 'Pro-ana versus Pro-recovery: A Content Analytic Comparison of Social Media Users' Communication about Eating Disorders on Twitter and Tumblr', *Frontiers in Psychology* Vol. 8 doi: 10.3389/fpsyg.2017.01356

Bronfenbrenner, U. (1979) *The Ecology of Human Development: Experiments by Nature and Design.* Cambridge, MA: Harvard University Press.

Callon, M. and Rabeharisoa, V. (2004) 'Gino's lesson on humanity: genetics, mutual entanglements and the sociologist's role', *Economy and Society* Vol. 33 (1) pp 1–27.

Cameron, L. and Matthews, R. (2017) 'More Than Pictures: Developing an Accessible Resource', *Tizard Learning Disability Review* Vol. 22 (2) pp 57–65.

Carpenter, J., Langan, J., Patsios, D. and Jepson, M. (2014) 'Deprivation of Liberty Safeguards: What Determines the Judgements of Best Interests Assessors? A Factorial Survey', *Journal of Social Work* Vol. 14 (6) pp 576–93.

Caton, S. and Landman, R. (2020) 'Internet Safety, Online Radicalisation and Young People with Learning Disabilities', *British Journal of Learning Disabilities* online 1–10 https://doi.org/10.1111/bld.123

Chadwick, D. D. (2019) 'Online Risk for People with Intellectual Disabilities', *Tizard Learning Disability Review* Vol. 24 (4) pp 180–87 https://doi. org/10.1108/TLDR-03-2019-0008

Chadwick, D. D., Chapman, M. and Caton, S. (2019) 'Digital Inclusion for People with an Intellectual Disability' in Attrill, A. A., Fullwood, C., Keep, M. and Kuss, D. (eds.) *Oxford Handbook of Cyberpsychology.* Oxford: Oxford University Press.

Cheswick, W., Bellovin, S. and Rubin, A. (2003) *Firewalls and Internet Security: Repelling the Wily Hacker.* London: Addison-Wesley Professional.

Cluley, V. (2017) 'From "Learning Disability to Intellectual Disability" – Perceptions of the Increasing Use of the Term "Intellectual Disability" in Learning Disability Policy, Research and Practice', *British Journal of Learning Disabilities* Vol. 46 pp 24–32.

Coyne, S., Rogers, A., Zurcher, J., Stockdale, L. and Booth, M. (2020) 'Does Time Spent Using Social Media Impact Mental Health?: An Eight Year Longitudinal Study', *Computers in Human Behaviour* Vol. 104 https://doi.org/10.1016/j.chb.2019.106160

Cresswell, T. (2004) *Place: A Short Introduction.* Oxford: Blackwell Publishing.

Csipke, E. and Horne, O. (2007) 'Pro-Eating Disorder Websites: Users' Opinions', *European Eating Disorders Review* Vol. 15 pp 196–206.

Custers, K. and Van den Bulck, J. (2009) 'Viewership of Pro-Anorexia Websites in Seventh, Ninth and Eleventh Graders', *European Eating Disorders Review* Vol. 17 pp 214–19.

Delgado, P., Avila, V., Fajardo, I. and Salmeron, L. (2019) 'Training Young Adults with Intellectual Disability to Read Critically on the Internet', *Journal of Applied Research in Intellectual Disabilities* Vol. 32 (3) pp 666–77 https://doi.org/10.1111/jar.12562

Department for Digital, Culture, Media and Sport (2016) *Child Safety Online: A Practical Guide for Providers of Social Media and Interactive Services* https://www.gov.uk/government/publications/child-safety-online-a-practical-guide-for-providers-of-social-media-and-interactive-services

Department of Health (2001) *Valuing People: A New Strategy for People with Learning Disabilities in the 21st Century*. London: The Stationery Office.

Department of Health (2005) *Mental Capacity Act*. London: HMSO.

Department of Health (2009) *Valuing People Now – A New Three-Year Strategy for People with Learning Disabilities*. London: The Stationery Office.

Department of Health and Social Care (2019) *Adult Social Care: Quality Matters action plan for year 2* https://www.gov.uk/government/publications/adult-social-care-quality-matters-action-plan-for-year-2

Department of Health (2000) *No Secrets: guidance on developing and implementing multi-agency policies and procedures to protect vulnerable adults form abuse.* https://www.gov.uk/government/publications/no-secrets-guidance-on-protecting-vulnerable-adults-in-care

DfE (2018) Keeping Children Safe in Education: Statutory Guidance for Schools and Colleges https://assets.publishing.service.gov.uk/government/uploads/system/ uploads/attachment_data/file/741314/Keeping_Children_Safe_in_Education__3_ September_2018_14.09.18.pdf

DfE (2019) *Relationships Education, Relationships and Sex Education (RSE) and Health Education* https://assets.publishing.service.gov.uk/government/uploads/system/uploads/attachment_data/file/908013/Relationships_Education__Relationships_and_Sex_Education__RSE__and_Health_Education.pdf

Dixon, D. R., Bergstrom, R., Smith, M. and Tarbox, J. (2010) 'A Review of Research on Procedures for Teaching Safety Skills to Persons with Developmental Disabilities', *Research in Developmental Disabilities* Vol. 31 (5) pp 985–94.

Durkheim, E. (1897) *Suicide, a Study in Sociology* (1951 edn., Spaulding, J. A. and G. Simpson trans.). London: Routledge.

Dyson, M. P., Hartling, L., Shulhan, J., Chisholm, A., Milne, A. and Sundar, P. (2016) 'A Systematic Review of Social Media Use to Discuss and View Deliberate Self-Harm Acts', *PLoS ONE* Vol. 11 (5) e0155813, https://doi.org/10.1371/journal.pone.0155813

Eleftheriou-Smith, L. (2014) 'Two Men convicted for Possessing Extreme "WhatsApp Porn" that Wasn't Viewed', *The Independent* https://www.independent.co.uk/life-style/gadgets-and-tech/two-men-convicted-for-possessing-extreme-whatsapp-porn-that-wasnt-viewed-9647507.html

European Court of Human Rights (1950) *The European Convention on Human Rights* https://www.echr.coe.int/Documents/Convention_ENG.pdf

European Union (2016) General Data Protection Regulation, https://eur-lex.europa.eu/legal-content/EN/ALL/

FCC (1996) Telecommunications Act of 1996, https://www.fcc.gov/general/telecommunications-act-1996

Federal Trade Commission (1998) *Childrens Online Privacy Protection Act* https://www.ftc.gov/enforcement/rules/rulemaking-regulatory-reform-proceedings/childrens-online-privacy-protection-rule

Flasher, J. (1978) 'Adultism', *Adolescence* Vol. 13 (51) pp 517–23.

Foucault, M. (1975) *Discipline and Punish* (A. Sheridan, trans.) Paris: Gallimard.

Friendly Wifi (online) *About Friendly Wifi* https://www.friendlywifi.com/about

Fyson, R. and Kitson, D. (2010) 'Human Rights and Social Wrongs: Issues in Safeguarding Adults with Learning Disabilities', *Practice* Vol. 22 (5) pp 319–20.

Gailey, J. A. (2009) 'Starving Is the Most Fun a Girl Can Have: The Pro-Ana Subculture as Edgework', *Critical Criminology* Vol. 17 pp 93–108.

Galis, V. (2011) 'Enacting Disability: How Can Science and Technology Studies Inform Disability Studies?', *Disability and Society* Vol. 26 (7) pp 825–38.

Giddens, A. (1990) *The Consequences of Modernity*. Cambridge: Polity.

Giddens, A. (1991) *Modernity and Self-Identity*. Cambridge: Polity.

Giles, D. (2006) 'Constructing Identities in Cyberspace: The Case of Eating Disorders', *British Journal of Social Psychology* Vol. 45 pp 463–77.

Gittens, D. (1998) *The Child in Question*. Basingstoke: Palgrave.

Goffman, E. (1959) *The Presentation of Self in Everyday Life*. Garden City, NY: Doubleday.

Goffman, E. (1963) *Stigna: Notes on the Management of a Spoiled Identity*. Penguin: Harmondsworth.

Gomart, E. and Hennion, A. (1999) 'A Sociology of Attachment: Music Amateurs, Drug Users' in Law, J. and Hassard, J. (eds.) *Actor Network Theory and After*. Oxford: Blackwell.

Graber, D. (2015) *Screen Time and Kids: Pediatricians Work on a New Prescription* http://www.huffingtonpost.com/diana-graber/screen-time-and-kids-pedi_b_8224342.html

Graham, M. (2016) 'Understanding of the Mental Capacity Act in work with older adults exploring the "unintended consequences" for service users' emotional wellbeing', *Working with Older People* Vol. 20 pp 151–6. 10.1108/WWOP-04-2016-0010.

Graham, M. and Cowley, J. (2015) *A Practical Guide to the Mental Capacity Act 2005: Putting the Principles of the Act into Practice*. London: Jessica Kingsley Publishers.

Grosvenor, I., Lohmann, I. and Mayer, C. (2009) 'Children and Youth at Risk: An Introduction' in Mayer, C., Lohmann, I. and Grosvenor, I. (eds.) *Children and Youth at Risk: Historical and International Perspectives*. Frankfurt am Main: Peter Lang.

Grimes, G. A., Hough, M. G., Mazur, E. and Signorella, M. L. (2010) 'Older Adults' Knowledge of Internet Hazards', *Educational Gerontology* Vol. 36 (3) pp 173–92.

Haas, S. M., Irr, M. E., Jennings, N. A. and Wagner, L. M. (2011) 'Communicating Thin: A Grounded Model of Online Negative Support Groups in the Pro-anorexia Movement', *New Media and Society* Vol. 13 (1) pp 40–57.

Harshbarger, J. L., Ahlers-Schmidt, C. R., Mayans, L., Mayans, D. and Hawkins, J. H. (2009) 'Pro-Anorexia Websites: What a Clinician Should Know', *International Journal Eating Disorders* Vol. 42 pp 367–70.

Hatton, C., Glover, G., Emerson, E. and Brown, I. (2016) *People with Learning disabilities in England 2015*. London: Public Health England.

Helm, T. and Rawnsley, A. (2018) *Health Chiefs to Set Social Media Time Limits for Young People* https://www.theguardian.com/media/2018/sep/29/health-chief-set-social-media-time-limits-young-people

Helsper, E. J. and Eynon, R. (2010) 'Digital Natives: Where Is the Evidence?', *British Educational Research Journal* Vol. 36 (3) pp 503–20.

Helsper, E. J. and Van Deursen, A. (2015) 'A Nuanced Understanding of Internet Use and Non-use Amongst Older Adults', *European Journal of Communication* Vol. 30 (2) pp 171–87.

Herring, J. (2016) *Vulnerable Adults and the Law*. Oxford: Oxford University Press.

Hollomotz, A. (2012) ' "A Lad Tried to Get Hold of My Boobs, So I Kicked Him": An Examination of Attempts by Adults with Learning Difficulties to Initiate Their Own Safeguarding', *Disability and Society* Vol. 27 (1) pp 117–29. https://doi.org/10.1080/09687599.2012.631801

Holmes, K. M. and O'Loughlin, N. (2012) 'The Experiences of People with Learning Disabilities on Social Networking Sites', *British Journal of Learning Disabilities* Vol. 42 p 307 https://doi.org/10.111/bid.12001

Horne, J. and Wiggins, S. (2009) Doing Being "On the Edge": Managing the Dilemma of Being Authentically Suicidal in an Online Forum', *Sociology of Health and Illness* Vol. 31 (92) pp 170–84.

House, A. (2020) 'Social Media, Self-harm and Suicide', *BJPsych Bulletin* Vol. 44 pp 131–3 https://doi.org/10.1192/bjb.2019.94

House of Commons Science and Technology Committee (2017) *Impact of Social Media and Screen-Use on Young People's Health* https://publications.parliament.uk/pa/cm201719/cmselect/cmsctech/822/822.pdf

Howard, J. W. (2019) 'Free Speech and Hate Speech', *Annual Review of Political Science* Vol. 22 pp 93–109.

Hutchby, I. (2001a) *Conversation and Technology from the Telephone to the Internet*. Cambridge: Polity.

Hutchby, I. (2001b) 'Technologies, Texts and Affordances', *Sociology* Vol. 35 (92) pp 441–56.

Hwang, J. M., Cheong, P. H. and Freely, T. H. (2009) 'Being Young and Feeling Blue in Taiwan: Examining Adolescent Depressive Mood and Online and Offline Activities', *New Media and Society* Vol. 11 (7) pp 1101–21.

Independent (2016) *School Calls Police Because Pupil Visited UKIP Website on Class Computer* https://www.independent.co.uk/news/uk/home-news/school-called-police-because-boy-visited-ukip-website-class-computer-a6899641.html

Independent Parliamentary Inquiry into Online Child Protection (2012) *Findings and Recommendations* http://www.safermedia.org.uk/Images/final-report.pdf

Internet Watch Foundation URL list (online) https://www.iwf.org.uk/our-technology/our-services/url-list/

James, A., Jenks, C. and Prout, A. (2010) *Theorizing Childhood.* Cambridge: Polity.

James, E., Morgan, H. and Mitchell, R. (2019) 'Innovating Adult Social Work Practice – Learning from the Named Social Worker for Adults with Learning Disabilities Pilots', *Social Work Education* Vol. 38 (4) pp 503–15 https://doi.org/10.1080/02615479.2018.1545833

Jenks, C. (2005) *Childhood* (2nd edn.) London: Routledge.

Jett, S., Laporte, D. and Wanchisn, J. (2010) 'Impact of Exposure to Pro-Eating Disorder Websites on Eating Behaviour in College Women', *European Eating Disorders Review: The Journal of the Eating Disorders Association* Vol. 18 pp 410–16.

Johnson, B. (2021) *Prime Ministers Questions*, 14 July [Hansard] (Vol. 699) https://hansard.parliament.uk/Commons/2021-07-14/debates/E0C07F8B-EE53-42B1-AEDE-1AA8CBFEFD4B/Engagements

Johnson, K. and Walmsley, J. (2010) *People with Intellectual Disabilities: Towards a Good Life?* Bristol: Policy Press.

Jorm, A. F. (2012) 'Mental Health Literacy: Empowering the Community to Take Action for Better Health', *Americal Psychologist* Vol. 67 (3) pp 131–243.

Jorm, A. F. (2019a) 'The Concept of Mental Health Literacy' in Okan, O., Bauer, U., Levin-Zamir, D., Pinheiro, P. and Sørensen, K. (eds.) *International Handbook of Health Literacy.* Bristol: Policy Press.

Jorm, A. F. (2019b) 'Mental Health Literacy Interventions in Adults' in Okan, O., Bauer, U., Levin-Zamir, D., Pinheiro, P. and Sørensen, K. (eds.) *International Handbook of Health Literacy.* Bristol: Policy Press.

Juarascio, A. S., Shaoib, A. and Timko, C. A. (2010) 'Pro-Eating Disorder Communities on Social Networking Sites: A Content Analysis', *Eating Disorders* Vol. 18 pp 393–407.

Kapur, N. and Goldney, R. (2019) *Suicide Prevention.* Oxford: Oxford University Press.

Karpowicz, E., Skärsäter, I. and Nevonen, L. (2009) 'Self-esteem in Patients Treated for Anorexia Nervosa', *International Journal of Mental Health Nursing* Vol. 18 pp 318–25.

Kirkwood, R. (2005) 'Support choice, support people: an argument for the study of pro-anorexia websites', *Atenea* Vol. 25 pp 117–29.

Lacohee, H., Crane, S. and Phippen, A. (2006) *Trustguide – A Final Report* https://s3.amazonaws.com/uploads.participedia.xyz/0321639c-b95b-42d8-86c9-2f6e6ee7436d_TrustGuide-final-Report.pdf

Latour, B. (1993) *We Have Never Been Modern*. Cambridge, MA: Harvard University Press.

Latour, B. (1994) 'Where Are the Missing Masses? The Sociology of a Few Mundane Artefacts' in Bijer, W. E. and Law, J. (eds.) *Shaping Technology/ Building Society: Studies in Sociotechnical Change*. Cambridge, MA: MIT Press.

Latour, B. (1999) 'On Recalling ANT' in Law, J. and Hassard, J. (eds.) *Actor Network Theory and After*. Oxford: Blackwell.

Lavis, A. and Winter, R. (2020) '#Online Harms or Benefits? An Ethnographic Analysis of the Positives and Negatives of Peer-support Around Self-harm on Social Media', *Journal of Child Psychology and Psychiatry* Vol. 61 (8) pp 842–54.

Law, J. (1991) 'Introduction: Monsters, Machines and Sociotechnical Relations' in Law, J. (ed.) *A Sociology of Monsters: Essays on Power, Technology and Domination*. London: Routledge.

Leaton Gray, S. and Phippen, A. (2017) *Invisibly Blighted The Digital Erosion of Childhood*. London: Institute of Education Press.

Lee, N. and Brown, S. (1994) 'Otherness and the Actor Network: The Undicovered Continent (Humans and Others: The Concept of "Agency" and Its Attribution)', *American Behavioural Scientist* Vol. 37 (6) pp 707–30.

Leo, J., Zitzelsberger, H., Zidenberg, A. and Edwards, C. (2018) 'Exploring the Impact of Enhancing Social Media Skills on Experiences of Social Inclusion Among Youth With and Without Disabilities', *Journal on Developmental Disabilities* Vol. 23 (2) pp 86–8.

Lessig, L. (2006) *Code Is Law / Code 2.0* https://www.socialtext.net/codev2/code_is_law

Levitas, R., Pantazis, C., Fahmy, E., Gordon, D., Lloyd, E. and Patsios, D. (2007) *The Multidimensional Analysis of Social Exclusion. Project Report*. Bristol: University of Bristol.

Ling, R. (2001) ' "We Release Them Little by Little": Maturation and Gender Identity as Seen in the Use of Mobile Telephony', *Personal and Ubiquitous Computing* Vol. 5 pp 123–36 https://doi.org/10.1109/ISTAS.1999.787348.

Ling, R. (2012) *Taken for Grantedness: The Embedding of Mobile Communication into Society*. London: MIT Press.

Livingstone, S. and Haddon, L. (2009) 'Introduction' in Livingstone, S. and Haddon, L. (eds.) *Kids Online: Opportunities and Risks for Children*. Bristol: Policy Press.

Lough, E. and Fisher, M. H. (2016) 'Internet Use and Online Safety in Adults with Williams Syndrome', *Journal of Intellectual Disability Research* Vol. 60 (10) pp 1020–30.

Lyle, A., Kemp, B., Spasova, A. and Gasper, U. (2016) 'Risks Related to Illegal Content in Cybercrime and Cyberterrorism Research' in Akhgar, B. and Brewster, B. (eds.) *Combatting Cybercrime and Cyberterrorism*. Cham, Switzerland: Springer.

Lyon, D. (2001) *Surveillance Society: Monitoring Everyday Life*. Buckingham: Open University Press.

Macintosh, I. (2019) *Wellbeing and the Web: Supporting Vulnerable People Online* https://scvo.scot/p/30110/2019/02/28/wellbeing-and-the-web-supporting-vulnerable-people-online

Marchant, A., Hawton, K., Stewart, A., Montgomery, P., Singaravelu, V., Lloyd, K., Purdy, N., Dane, K. and John, A. (2017) 'A Systematic Review of the Relationship Between Internet Use, Self-harm and Suicidal Behaviour in Young People: The Good, the Bad and the Unknown', *PLoS ONE* Vol. 12 (8) e0181722, https:// doi.org/10.1371/journal.pone.0181722

Martin, C., Hope, S., Zubairi, S. and Ipsos MORI Scotland (2016) *The Role of Digital Exclusion in Social Exclusion*, Carnegie UK Trust, https://d1ssu070pg2v9i.cloudfront.net/pex/carnegie_uk_trust/2016/09/LOW-2697-CUKT-Digital-Participation-Report-REVISE.pdf

Massey, D. (2005) *For Space*. London: Sage.

Matthewman, S. (2011) *Technology and Social Theory*. Basingstoke: Palgrave.

McManus, S., Gunnel, D., Cooper, C., Bebbington, P., Howard, L., Brugha, T., Jenkins, R., Hassiotis, A., Weich, S. and Appleyby, L. (2019a) 'Prevalence of Non-suicidal Self-harm and Service Contact in England, 2000–2104: Repeated Cross-sectional Surveys of General Population', *The Lancet Psychiatry* Vol. 6 (7) pp 573–81.

McManus, S., Lubian, K., Bennett, C., Turley, C., Porter, L., Gill, V., with Gunnell, D. and Weich, S. (2019b) *Suicide and Self- harm in Britain: Researching Risk and Resilience Using UK Surveys – Summary*. NatCen: London, https://www.rcpsych.ac.uk/docs/default-source/improving-care/nccmh/suicide-prevention/monthly-clinic/(5a)-suicide-and-self-harm-in-britain-summary-report-natcen.pdf

McTernan, N. and Ryan, F. (2020) *The Harmful Impact of Suicide and Self-harm Content Online: A Review of the Literature*. Ireland, National Suicide Research Foundation, https://www.nsrf.ie/wp-content/uploads/2020/11/Harmful-impact-of-suicide-and-self-harm-content-online-Review-of-the-literature-Final.pdf

Mellor, P. A. and Shilling, C. (1997) *Re-forming the Body*. London: Sage.

Mental Health Foundation (2021) *Self-harm* https://www.mentalhealth.org. uk/a-to-z/s/self-harm

Mohdin, A. (2019) 'Matt Hancock "Won't Rule Out" Compulsory Vaccinations', *The Guardian* https://www.theguardian.com/ politics/2019/may/04/matt-hancock-wont-rule-out-compulsory-vaccinations

Morris, S. (2020) 'Chairman of Aintree Racecourse Killed Herself, Coroner Rules', *The Guardian* 22 September, https://www.theguardian.com/uk-news/ 2020/sep/22/chairman-of-aintree-racecourse-killed-herself-coroner-rules

Moser, I. (2010) 'Against Normalisation: Subverting Norms of Ability and Disability', *Science as Culture* Vol. 9 (2) pp 201–40.

Moser, I and Law, J. (1999) 'Good passages, bad passages' in Law, J. and Hassard, J, (eds.) *Actor Network Theory and After*. Oxford: Blackwell.

NBC News (2005) *Pro-anorexia Movement Has Cult-like Appeal* http://www. nbcnews.com/id/8045047/ns/health-mental_health/t/pro-anorexia-movement-has-cult-like-appeal/#.V1aZB2Mld-U

NHS (n.d.) *A Health and Care Digital Capability Framework* https://www. hee.nhs.uk/sites/default/files/documents/Digital%20Literacy%20 Capability%20Framework%202018.pdf

OFCOM (2019) *Children and Parents Media Use and Attitudes report* https:// www.ofcom.org.uk/__data/assets/pdf_file/0023/190616/children-media-use-attitudes-2019-report.pdf :

Ofsted (2018) *School Inspection Handbook: Handbook for Inspecting Schools in England under Section 5 of the Education Act 2005* https://assets.publishing. service.gov.uk/government/uploads/system/uploads/ attachment_data/ file/730127/School_inspection_handbook_section_5_270718.pdf

Oksanen, A., Näsi, M., Minkkinen, J., Keipi, T., Kaakinen, M. and Räsänen, P. (2016) 'Young People Who Access Harm-advocating Online Content: A Four-country Survey', *Cyberpsychology: Journal of Psychosocial Research on Cyberspace* Vol. 10 (2) https://doi.org/10.5817/CP2016-2-6

ONS (2020) *Suicides in England and Wales: 2019 Registrations* https://www. ons.gov.uk/peoplepopulationandcommunity/birthsdeathsandmarriages/ deaths/bulletins/suicidesintheunitedkingdom/2019registrations

Orben, A. and Przybylski, A. K. (2019) 'Screens, Teens, and Psychological Well-Being: Evidence From Three Time-Use-Diary Studies', *Psychological Science* Vol. 30 (5) pp. 682–96.

O'Reilly, T. (2009) *What Is web 2.0*. California: O'Reilly Media.

Ottmann, G., McVilly, K. and Maragoudaki, M. (2016) '"I Walk from Trouble": Exploring Safeguards with Adults with Intellectual Disabilities – An Australian Qualitative Study', *Disability & Society* Vol. 31 (1) pp 47–63 https://doi.org/10.1080/09687599.2015.1122575

Overmars-Marx, T., Thomése, F., Verdonschot, M. and Meininger, H. (2014) 'Advancing Social Inclusion in the Neighbourhood for People with an Intellectual Disability: An Exploration of the Literature', *Disability and Society* Vol. 29 (2) pp 255–74.

PacerMonitor (online) *Robbins v Lower Merion District* https://www.pacermonitor.com/view/6LZS7RA/ROBBINS_et_al_v_LOWER_MERION_SCHOOL_DISTRICT_et__paedce-10-00665__0001.0.pdf

Pawson, R. and Tilley, N. (1997) *Realistic Evaluation*. London: Sage.

Perry Barlow, J. (1996) *Declaration of Independence for Cyberspace* https://www.eff.org/cyberspace-independence

Phippen, A. (2009) *Sharing Personal Images and Videos Among Young People' Report for South West Grid for Learning* http://webfronter.com/surreymle/devonesafety/other/Sexting%20report%20-%20andy%20phippen.pdf

Phippen, A. (2016) *Online Children's Online Behaviour and Safety – Policy and Rights Challenges*. Basingstoke: Palgrave.

Phippen, A. and Bond, E. (2019a) *Police Response to Youth Offending Around the Generation and Distribution of Indecent Images of Children and its Implications.* Ipswich: University of Suffolk https://www.uos.ac.uk/sites/default/files/FOI-Report-Final-Outcome-21.pdf

Phippen, A. and Bond, E. (2019b) 'The Online Harms Spearmint Paper – Just More Doing More?', *Entertainment Law Review* Vol. 30 (6) pp 169–73.

Phippen, A. and Bond, E. (2020) 'Online Safeguarding of Adults with Mental Capacity Issues – Are the 3 Cs the Most Progressive Response?', *Entertainment Law Review* Vol. 31 (1) pp 8–13.

Phippen, A. and Bond, E. (2021) 'Virtually Vulnerable: Why Technology Challenges the Fundamental Concepts of Vulnerability and Risk' in Addidle, G. and Liddle, J. (eds.) *Public Management and Vulnerability: Contextualising Change*. London: Routledge.

Phippen, A. and Brennan, M. (2020) *Sexting and Revenge Pornography: Legislative and Social Dimensions of a Modern Digital Phenomenon*. London: Routledge.

Pilgrim, D. (2020) *Key Concepts in Mental Health*. London: Sage.

Politico (2021) *French Regulator Issues Age Verification Ultimatum to Porn Sites* https://www.politico.eu/article/french-regulator-issues-age-verification-ultimatum-to-porn-sites/

Power, A. and Bartlett, R. (2018) ' "I Shouldn't Be Living There Because I Am a Sponger": Negotiating Everyday Geographies by People with Learning Disabilities', *Disability and Society* Vol. 33 (4) pp 562–78. https://doi.org/10.1080/09687599.2018.1436039

Prensky, M. (2001) 'Digital Natives, Digital Immigrants', *On the Horizon* Vol. 9 (5) pp. 1–6.

Prout, A. (1996) 'Actor-network Theory, Technology and Medical Sociology: An Illustrative Analysis of the Metered Dose Inhaler', *Sociology of Health and Illness* Vol. 18 (2) pp 198–219.

Przybylski, A. K. and Weinstein, N. (2017) 'A Large-Scale Test of the Goldilocks Hypothesis: Quantifying the Relations Between Digital-Screen Use and the Mental Well-Being of Adolescents', *Psychological Science* Vol. 28 (2) pp 204–15.

Public Health England (2020) *Research and Analysis Chapter 5: Adult Social Care* https://www.gov.uk/government/publications/people-with-learning-disabilities-in-england/chapter-5-adult-social-care#people-with-learning-disabilities-in-england

Ramsten, C., Martin, L., Dag, M. and Marmatål Hammar, L. (2019) 'A Balance of Social Inclusion and Risks: Staff Perceptions of Information and Communication Technology in the Daily Life of Young Adults with Mild to Moderate Intellectual Disability in a Social Care Setting', *Journal of Policy and Practice in Intellectual Disabilities* Advance Online Publication https://doi.org/10.1111/jppi.12278

Reavley, N. J. and Jorm, A. F. (2011) 'The Quality of Mental Disorder Information Websites: A Review', *Patient Education and Counselling* Vol. 85 (2) pp 16–25.

Reidenberg, J. (1997) 'Lex Informatica: The Formulation of Information Policy Rules through Technology', *Texas Law Review* Vol. 76 p 553.

Rich, E. (2006) 'Anorexic Dis(connection): Managing Anorexia as an Illness and an Identity', *Sociology of Health and Illness* Vol. 28 (3) pp 234–305.

Rogers, C. (2016) 'Intellectual Disability and Sexuality: On the Agenda?', *Sexualities* Vol. 19 (5–6) pp 617–22.

Ross, M., Grossmann, I. and Schryer, E. (2014) 'Contrary to Psychological and Popular Opinion, There Is No Compelling Evidence that Older Adults Are Disproportionately Victimized by Consumer Fraud', *Perspectives on Psychological Science* Vol. 9 (4) 427–42.

Royal College of Psychiatrists (2020) *Self-harm and Suicide in Adults: Final Report of the Patient Safety Group* https://www.rcpsych.ac.uk/docs/default-source/improving-care/better-mh-policy/college-reports/college-report-cr229-self-harm-and-suicide.pdf?sfvrsn=b6fdf395_10

Samaritans (2020) *Understanding Self-harm and Suicide Content Online* https://media.samaritans.org/documents/Understanding_self-harm_and_suicide_content_online_FINAL.pdf

Schaubert, V. (2019) *My Disabled Son's Amazing Gaming Life in the World of Warcraft* https://www.bbc.co.uk/news/disability-47064773

Schneier, B. (2016) *The Eternal Value of Privacy* https://www.wired.com/2006/05/the-eternal-value-of-privacy

Sentencing Council (2018) *Overarching Principles: Domestic Abuse Definitive Guideline* https://www.sentencingcouncil.org.uk/wp-content/uploads/Overarching-Principles-Domestic-Abuse-definitive-guideline-Web.pdf

Sergeant, M. (2009) 'Safeguarding Vulnerable Adults' Liberty: The Law', *Learning Disability Practice* Vol. 12 (4) pp 16–20.

Setty, E. (2020) *Risk and Harm in Youth Sexting: Young People's Perspectives.* London: Routledge.

Shanahan, N., Brennan, C. and House, A. (2019) 'Self- harm and Social Media: Thematic Analysis of Images Posted on Three Social Media Sites', *BMJ Open* Vol. 9 e027006 https://doi.org/10.1136/ bmjopen-2018-027006

Sharratt, E. (2020) 'Report Harmful Content Pilot Year Evaluation' https:// d1xsi6mgo67kia.cloudfront.net/uploads/2021/10/rhc-report-final-with-logos.pdf

Slater, M. (2017) *Crime, Justice and Social Media.* London: Routledge.

Stevens, I. and Hassett, P. (2007) 'Applying Complexity Theory to Risk in Relation to Child Protection Practice', *Childhood* Vol. 14 (1) pp 128–44.

Strathern, M. (1999) 'What Is Intellectual Property After?' in Law, J. and Hassard, J. (eds.) *Actor Network Theory and After.* Oxford: Blackwell.

Summers, C. A., Smith, R. W. and Walker Reczek, R. (2016) 'An Audience of One: Behaviorally Targeted Ads as Implied Social Labels', *Journal of Consumer Research* Vol. 43 (1) pp 156–78.

The Times (2018) 'Time Limits for Children Hooked on Social Media' https://www.thetimes.co.uk/article/time-limits-for-children-hooked-on-social-media-3s66vwgct

Thompson, D. (2019) 'Commentary: The Internet, Social Media, Relationships and Sex', *Tizard Learning Disability Review* Vol. 24 (1) pp 20–3.

Tiller, J. M., Sloane, G., Schmidt, U. and Troop, N. (1997) 'Social Support in Patients with Anorexia Nervosa and Bulimia Nervosa', *International Journal of Eating Disorders* Vol. 21 31–8.

Tindall, B. (2015) *Decisions to Safeguard Adults with Learning Disabilities Can Make Them Less Safe* https://www.communitycare.co.uk/2015/04/21/decisions-safeguard-adults-learning-disabilities-can-make-less-safe/

Top 10 VPN (2019) *Collateral Damage in the War Against Online Harms* https://www.openrightsgroup.org/publications/collateral-damage-in-the-war-against-online-harms/

UK Government (1978) Protection of Children Act 1978, https://www.legislation.gov.uk/ukpga/1978/37/section/1

UK Government (2000) Regulation of Investigatory Powers Act 2000, section 49, https://www.legislation.gov.uk/ukpga/2000/23/section/49

UK Government (2003) Sexual Offences Act 2003, http://www.legislation.gov.uk/ukpga/2003/42/pdfs/ukpga_20030042_en.pdf

UK Government (2005) Mental Capacity Act 2005, section 1, http://www.legislation.gov.uk/ukpga/2005/9/section/1/2015-10-01

UK Government (2013a) *The Internet and Pornography: Prime Minister Calls for Action* https://www.gov.uk/government/speeches/the-internet-and-pornography-prime-minister-calls-for-action

UK Government (2013b) *Mental Capacity Act Code of Practice* https://www. gov.uk/government/publications/mental-capacity-act-code-of-practice

UK Government (2014) Care Act 2014, http://www.legislation.gov.uk/ ukpga/2014/23/contents/enacted

UK Government (2015a) Serious Crime Act 2015, http://www.legislation. gov.uk/ukpga/2015/9/section/67/enacted

UK Government (2015b) *Protecting Children from Radicalisation: The Prevent Duty* https://www.gov.uk/government/publications/protecting-children-from-radicalisation-the-prevent-duty

UK Government (2017) Digital Economy Act 2017, Part 3, http://www. legislation.gov.uk/ukpga/2017/30/part/3/enacted

UK Government (2018) Data Protection Act 2018, https://www.legislation. gov.uk/ukpga/2018/12/contents/enacted

UK Government (2019) *Online Harms White Paper* https://assets.publishing. service.gov.uk/government/uploads/system/uploads/attachment_data/ file/793360/Online_Harms_White_Paper.pdf

UK Government (2021a) Draft Online Safety Bill, https://www.gov.uk/ government/publications/draft-online-safety-bill

UK Government (2021b) *Landmark Laws to Keep Children Safe, Stop Racial Hate and Protect Democracy Online Published* https://www.gov.uk/ government/news/landmark-laws-to-keep-children-safe-stop-racial-hate-and-protect-democracy-online-published

UK Safer Internet Centre (2015) *1st Anniversary of the Digital Friendly WiFi Accreditation Scheme* https://www.saferinternet.org.uk/blog/ 1st-anniversary-digital-friendly-wifi-accreditation-scheme

UK Safer Internet Centre (2020) *New data: thousands of schools need more help to tackle online safety effectively* https://www.saferinternet.org.uk/blog/new-data-thousands-schools-need-more-help-tackle-online-safety-effectively

UK Safer Internet Centre (2021a) *Appropriate Filtering* https://www. saferinternet.org.uk/advice-centre/teachers-and-school-staff/appropriate-filtering-and-monitoring/appropriate-filtering

UK Safer Internet Centre (2021b) *Appropriate Monitoring* https://www. saferinternet.org.uk/advice-centre/teachers-and-school-staff/appropriate-filtering-and-monitoring/appropriate-monitoring

UK Safer Internet Centre, Office of the Australian eSafety Commissioner and Netsafe New Zealand (2017) *Young People and Sexting – Attitudes and Behaviours: Research Findings from the UK, New Zealand and Australia* https:// www.netsafe.org.nz/wp-content/uploads/2017/12/Young_people_and_ sexting_Attitudes_and_behaviours.pdf

UKCCIS (2016) *Child Safety Online: A Practical Guide for Providers of Social Media and Interactive Services* https://www.gov.uk/government/uploads/ system/uploads/attachment_data/file/487973/ukccis_guide-final__3_.pdf

United Nations (1989) Convention on the Rights of the Child, https://www.ohchr.org/Documents/ProfessionalInterest/crc.pdf

United Nations (2006) Convention of the Rights of Persons with Disabilities, https://www.un.org/development/desa/disabilities/convention-on-the-rights-of-persons-with-disabilities/convention-on-the-rights-of-persons-with-disabilities-2.html

United Nations (2016) *The Promotion, Protection and Enjoyment of Human Rights on the Internet* https://undocs.org/A/HRC/32/L.20

United Nations Human Rights Council (2018) *Special Rapporteur on the Promotion and Protection of Freedom of Opinion and Expression* https://www.ohchr.org/en/issues/freedomopinion/pages/opinionindex.aspx

Uzelac, A. (2008) 'How to Understand Digital Culture: A Resource for a Knowledge Society?' in Uzelac, A. and Cvjetičanin, B. (eds.) *Digital Culture: The Changing Dynamics.* Zagreb: Institute for International Relations.

Van Deursen, A. J. and van Dijk, J. A. (2009) 'Improving Digital Skills for the Use of Online Public Information and Services', *Government Information Quarterly* Vol. 26 (2) pp 333–40.

Van Deursen, A. and Van Dijk, J. (2011) 'Internet Skills and the Digital Divide', *New Media and Society* Vol. 13 (6) pp 893–911.

Van Deursen A. and Van Dijk J. (2014) 'The Digital Divide Shifts to Differences in Usage', *New Media & Society* Vol. 16 (3) pp 507–26.

Van Wilsem, J. (2013) '"Bought It, But Never Got It": Assessing Risk Factors for Online Consumer Fraud Victimization', *European Sociological Review* Vol. 29 (2) pp 168–78.

Vitis, L. and Gilmour, F. (2016) 'Dic Pics on Blast: A Woman's Resistance to Online Sexual Harassment Using Humour, Art and Instagram', *Crime Media Culture* Vol 13 (3) pp 1–21 https://doi.org/10.1177/1741659016652445

Warner, L. (2008) 'Get a New Media Life!', *Learning Disability Practice* Vol. 11 (9) pp 26–7.

Watt, G. and Brazier, L. (2009) 'Safeguarding Vulnerable adults' Liberty: Creating a New Role', *Learning Disability Practice* Vol. 12 (8) pp 18–21.

Westerlund, M., Hadlaczky, G. and Wasserman, D. (2016) 'Case Study of Posts Before and After a Suicide on a Swedish Internet Forum', *The British Journal of Psychiatry* Vol. 207 pp 476–82 https://doi.org/10.1192/bjp.bp.114.154484

White, P. and Forrester-Jones, R. (2020) 'Valuing e-inclusion: Social Media and the Social Networks of Adolescents with Intellectual Disability', *Journal of Intellectual Disabilities* Vol. 24 (3) pp 381–97.

Wikipedia (online) *The Scunthorpe Problem* https://en.wikipedia.org/wiki/Scunthorpe_problem

Yar, M. (2006) *Cybercrime and Society.* London: Sage.

Legal rulings

[2016] EWHC 3473 (Fam). https://www.bailii.org/ew/cases/EWHC/Fam/2016/3473.html

[2018] EWFC 47. https://www.bailii.org/ew/cases/EWFC/HCJ/2018/47.html

[2019] EWCOP 2. Re: A (Capacity: Social Media and Internet Use: Best Interests). https://www.bailii.org/ew/cases/EWCOP/2019/2.html

[2019] EWCOP 3. Re: B (Capacity: Social Media: Care and Contact). https://www.bailii.org/ew/cases/EWCOP/2019/3.html

[2019] EWCA Civ 913. https://www.bailii.org/ew/cases/EWCA/Civ/2019/913.html

[2019] EWCOP 55. https://www.bailii.org/ew/cases/EWCOP/2019/57.html

[2019] EWCOP 64. https://www.bailii.org/ew/cases/EWCOP/2019/64.html

[2019] EWCOP 66. Re: AB (Court of Protection: Police Disclosure). https://www.bailii.org/ew/cases/EWCOP/2019/66.html

[2020] EWCOP 24. https://www.bailii.org/ew/cases/EWCOP/2020/24.html

[2020] EWCOP 29. https://www.bailii.org/ew/cases/EWCOP/2020/29.html

[2020] EWCOP 32. https://www.bailii.org/ew/cases/EWCOP/2020/32.html

[2020] EWCOP 43. https://www.bailii.org/ew/cases/EWCOP/2020/43.html

[2020] EWHC 139 (Fam). https://www.bailii.org/ew/cases/EWHC/Fam/2020/139.html

[2021] EWCOP 20. https://www.bailii.org/ew/cases/EWCOP/2021/20.html

Index

References to figures appear in *italic* type;
those in **bold** type refer to tables.